PRO-LIFE REFLECTIONS
FOR EVERY DAY

"Let it be done to me according to Your word . . ." (Lk 1:38).

PRO-LIFE REFLECTIONS FOR EVERY DAY

MINUTE MEDITATIONS FOR EVERY DAY
CONTAINING A TEXT FROM SCRIPTURE
(OR OTHER CHURCH DOCUMENTS),
A REFLECTION, AND A PRAYER

By
Father Frank Pavone

Illustrated

CATHOLIC BOOK PUBLISHING CORP.
New Jersey

CONTENTS

NIHIL OBSTAT: Rev. Msgr. James M. Cafone, M.A., S.T.D.
Censor Librorum

IMPRIMATUR: ✠ Most Rev. John J. Myers, J.C.D., D.D.
Archbishop of Newark

(T-168)

ISBN 978-0-89942-168-1

INTRODUCTION

JESUS Christ is Life. To stand with Him is to stand with life and to stand against whatever destroys life. Being "pro-life" in our convictions, words, and actions is not merely a "personal belief" or a political ideology. Pro-life action is not merely a hobby or an "extracurricular" activity.

Pro-life is a spirituality, a way of relating to God, an integral dimension of the Christian Gospel. There is, in the end, only one Gospel. It is the Gospel of Jesus Christ, which is the Gospel of Life.

Pro-life Reflections for Every Day is meant to immerse us, day by day, in the spirituality of pro-life. At Priests for Life (also known as Missionaries of the Gospel of Life), we have developed and articulated this spirituality since 1991. It is a spirituality that draws deeply from the lives and teachings of three great pro-life warriors whom I was privileged to know personally and work with in the pro-life arena: Pope John Paul II, Mother Teresa of Calcutta, and Cardinal John O'Connor.

It is, moreover, a spirituality that is Biblical, Prophetic, Liturgical, Eucharistic, Ecumenical, and Marian. It is marked by a spirit of joy, a serene confidence, a deep compassion, a radical solidarity with the vulnerable, a strong courage, a constant readiness for public witness, and a passion for justice.

This is the spirit which you will find in these daily meditations, most of which take their starting point from Scripture, and which also draw from Pope John Paul II's 1995 encyclical, *The Gospel of Life,* as well as from other documents of the Magisterium, from liturgical texts, and from writings of the saints.

The reflections, moreover, are not just to help us meditate but to inspire us to act. Prayer and action cannot be divorced, and therefore these reflections are as much of an action plan as a teaching, and as much of a commission as a prayer.

And as you pray the *Pro-life Reflections for Every Day* with me through the course of the year, know that countless pro-life believers are doing the same. Let's pray for each other; let's work together to build a Culture of Life; and let's look forward to the victory!

Fr. Frank Pavone

National Director, Priests for Life

National Pastoral Director,
Rachel's Vineyard Ministries
President, National Pro-life Religious Council

AM the Alpha and the Omega, the **JAN.** Beginning and the End.

—Rev 21:6

1

REFLECTION. God gives us the gift of life, in units of years and months and days, and we likewise give it back to Him, in days and months and years of faithful service.

In the New Year, let us put the defense of the unborn at the top of our priority list.

PRAYER. *Lord, enable me to devote more time, energy, and resources to the greatest human rights movement of our day, the pro-life movement.*

 HEN you hold a banquet, invite the **JAN.** poor, the crippled, the lame, and the blind. Then indeed will you be blessed because they have no way to repay you. —Lk 14:13-14

2

REFLECTION. Jesus calls us to the purest form of love, that is, love of those who cannot repay us. The unborn children, whose lives we seek to protect, cannot repay us and do not even know we are fighting for them.

Pro-life work is motivated by pure love.

PRAYER. *Lord, increase my love for the children in the womb who cannot acknowledge or repay me. May You be my only reward.*

HOEVER does not take up his own cross and follow Me cannot be My disciple. —Lk 14:27

JAN. 3

REFLECTION. To stand up for what is right means we stand against what is wrong, and that means that those who love what is wrong will oppose us, just as they opposed Christ.

Taking up the cross means we continue standing for the right even when that opposition comes.

PRAYER. *Lord, thank You for the grace of being pro-life and of standing strong when others ridicule or oppose me. May Your peace fill my soul, and may I become more like Your crucified and risen Son.*

 T IS more important than ever that we have the will to honestly face the truth and say exactly what it is. —*The Gospel of Life*, 58

JAN. 4

REFLECTION. Some call abortion "termination of pregnancy." But so is birth. The fact is that every pregnancy terminates. The issue is how.

Abortion supporters are simply masking an act of violence with their language.

PRAYER. *Spirit of truth, keep us free from the power of deception. Give us clear minds to know truth and courageous tongues to speak it.*

T IS a supreme injustice and arbitrariness when some make themselves the judges of who should live and who should die.

JAN. 5

—*The Gospel of Life*, 66

REFLECTION. When people ask me about the right to die, I say, "Don't worry—you won't miss out on it." A right is a moral claim. We do not have a claim on death; it has a claim on us!

It is our duty to surround our dying brothers and sisters with all the love and care we can.

PRAYER. *Lord Jesus, You conquered the power of death. May we seek freedom from its power only in You!*

 AKE this and eat; this is My Body.

JAN. 6

—Mt 26:26

REFLECTION. Supporters of abortion say, "This is my body, I can do what I want." Jesus says, "This is My Body, given up for you." The same words are spoken from opposite ends of the universe with totally opposite results.

Let us resolve to live those words as Jesus did, giving ourselves away for the good of others, born and unborn.

PRAYER. *Lord, thank You for my body, my life, and my freedom. May all of us understand the purpose of these gifts: to freely give ourselves away in love just as You did.*

TURN my thoughts in particular to you, women who have had abortions . . . Do not despair or abandon hope.

JAN. 7

—*The Gospel of Life*, 99

REFLECTION. The God of Life is a God of Mercy. The pro-life movement rejects abortion, but does not reject those who have abortions.

Rather, it embraces them with love and mercy, and invites them to the forgiveness and peace of Christ.

PRAYER. *Lord, I pray for all those who have had abortions. Through the compassion of others, may they turn to You for forgiveness, and may You grant them Your peace.*

 CONSISTENT ethic of life . . . far from . . . equating all issues touching on the dignity of human life—recognizes instead the distinctive character of each issue while giving each its proper place within a coherent moral vision.

JAN. 8

—US Bishops' Pastoral Plan for Pro-life Activities, 2001

REFLECTION. The fundamental pro-life principle is that we never target the innocent.

War and capital punishment are never justified if they do, whereas abortion is never successful if it doesn't.

PRAYER. *Lord, give us a consistent respect for every life and a proper understanding of every life issue.*

EOPLE brought children to Him so that
He might lay His hands on them and
pray. The disciples rebuked them, but
Jesus said, "Let the little children come
to me, and do not hinder them."

**JAN.
9**

—Mt 19:13-14

REFLECTION. The Apostles mistakenly thought
that Jesus didn't have time for the children, that
they were not important enough for His attention, that they were a distraction from His mission.

Instead, Jesus indicates that they are at the
heart of His mission.

PRAYER. *Lord, the kingdom belongs to children.
Grant that we may treat them accordingly.*

HEY shed innocent blood, the blood of
their sons and their daughters, whom
they sacrificed to the idols of Canaan,
polluting the land with their blood.

**JAN.
10**

—Ps 106:38

REFLECTION. The killing of children is especially condemned by God through the Prophets. In
the land God gave His people to occupy, foreign
nations had the custom of sacrificing some of
their children in fire.

God told His people that they were not to
share in this sin. Sadly, however, they did so.

PRAYER. *Have mercy on us, Lord, and save us
from the idolatry of death.*

11

ITH humility and confidence, open your hearts to repentance. Your merciful Father awaits you, so he can give you His pardon and peace.
—John Paul II to those who have had abortions . . . *The Gospel of Life*, 99

JAN.
11

REFLECTION. Every day around the world, men and women who have lost children to abortion gather for Rachel's Vineyard retreats.

These provide an opportunity to face the wounds of abortion in a safe, affirming environment of prayer and the support of others who have been through the same experience.

PRAYER. *Lord, be with all those who are going through healing after abortion, and bring them quickly to Your peace.*

OD created human beings in His own image, in the image of God He created them; male and female He created them.
—Gen 1:27

JAN.
12

REFLECTION. It is only of God that the word "create" is used, because only He is the one Who can bring life out of nothing. The sanctity of life has its root in the unique relationship that human beings have with their Creator.

Life is sacred because it comes from God, belongs to God, and returns to God.

PRAYER. *Thank You Father of Life, for creating every human being, born and unborn, healthy and sick.*

ND I will put enmity between you and the Woman, and between your offspring and hers; He will crush your head, and you will strike His heel.

—Gen 3:15

REFLECTION. Life is victorious over death. This is one of Scripture's most basic themes. The victory of life is foretold in the promise that the head of the serpent, through whom death entered the world, would be crushed.

The promise is fulfilled when a mother, Mary, gives birth to a child, Christ, Who destroys death.

PRAYER. *Lord, renew my confidence today that Your promise to us will continue to be fulfilled as Your Kingdom of Life grows in the world.*

 WO blind men . . . shouted, "Lord, Son of David, take pity on us." The crowd rebuked them and told them to be silent. . . . Jesus stopped and called them, saying, "What do you want Me to do for you?"

—Mt 20:30-32

REFLECTION. Jesus always broke through the false levels of privilege that people around Him set up.

Somehow the crowd thought the blind men weren't worth Jesus' attention. And so the crowd told them to keep quiet. But Jesus gave them His attention and care.

PRAYER. *Lord, You teach us to see beyond appearances, prejudices, and false distinctions. Help us care for every life, born and unborn.*

I N Him we live and move and have our being.
—Acts 17:28

JAN. 15

REFLECTION. Dr. Martin Luther King, Jr., fought for the equal dignity of every human life. "If we are to have peace on earth," he wrote, "we must be concerned about . . . the sacredness of all human life. Man is a child of God, made in His image, and must be respected as such.

"When we truly believe this," he continued, "we won't kill anybody."

PRAYER. *Lord, thank You for the privilege of defending human life through the pro-life movement.*

T HEY have conquered him by the blood of the Lamb and by the word of their testimony.
—Rev 12:11

JAN. 16

REFLECTION. At the March for Life in Washington, women who have had abortions march at the very beginning of the immense crowd and carry signs that say, "I Regret My Abortion." Later they gather at the steps of the Supreme Court and share their testimonies one by one.

Fathers of aborted babies are also there with signs saying, "I Regret Lost Fatherhood."

PRAYER. *Lord, bless these courageous men and women. Thank You for their powerful witness.*

STAND firm and immovable, devoting yourselves completely to the work of the Lord. —1 Cor 15:58a

JAN.
17

REFLECTION. A young girl wrote: "My mother and I are taking a bus and will be coming to the March for Life. My teacher said that I will receive zeros on any work that I miss, and it can't be made up.

"I told her missing a day at school in order to stand up for life is more important, and I'm willing to suffer the consequences."

PRAYER. *Lord, may we imitate this young girl's willingness to sacrifice for the cause of life!*

MANY Christians . . . are jointly involved in bold projects aimed at changing the world by inculcating respect for the rights and needs of everyone, especially . . . the defenseless.

JAN.
18

—John Paul II, *Ut Unum Sint*, 43

REFLECTION. From January 18 to the 25th, the Week of Prayer for Christian Unity is observed. All Christians, by definition, acknowledge Jesus as Lord and Savior of the world. That affirmation of Christ requires that we work to fight injustice.

The pro-life movement continues to be the arena where these efforts are most visible and valuable.

PRAYER. *Lord Jesus, may we be one as You and Your Father are one.*

I WILL praise Your name, O Lord . . . for You have rescued me.

—Ps 54:8-9

JAN.
19

REFLECTION. Norma McCorvey, the plaintiff in the Roe v. Wade decision that legalized abortion, agreed to let her name be used in a case she hardly understood, so that the case would have a better chance. She never did have an abortion.

Now, Norma is completely pro-life and works to end abortion.

PRAYER. *Lord, I thank You for Norma's conversion, a sign of hope for our culture.*

 PUT an end to the malice of the wicked but continue to sustain the righteous.

—Ps 7:10

JAN.
20

REFLECTION. Doe v. Bolton is the Supreme Court's companion case to Roe v. Wade, issued on the same day, January 22, 1973. It expanded the definition of health so widely that no abortion could be prohibited in practice.

The plaintiff in Doe, Sandra Cano, who has always been against abortion, was deceived into participating in this case and now works to get this decision reversed.

PRAYER. *Lord, send Your blessings upon Sandra, and upon all who work for the reversal of these disastrous decisions of our Court.*

16

N the Lord your labor is not in vain.

JAN.
21

—1 Cor 15:58b

REFLECTION. Every January tens of thousands of Americans participate in the annual March for Life in Washington, DC, or the annual West Coast Walk for Life in San Francisco.

These events give public witness to the fact that most Americans want to see unborn children protected, and enable all who participate to be renewed in their convictions and determination to work for that protection.

PRAYER. *Lord, bless all those who will march this year for life, and the many more who labor for life in their own communities every day.*

 HE Lord is the Judge of the nations.

JAN.
22

—Ps 7:9

REFLECTION. On January 22, 1973, the decision called Roe v. Wade, that legalized abortion, was handed down by the US Supreme Court.

Today, in churches and on streets all over America, people of all ethnic backgrounds and faiths are praying and protesting that decision.

PRAYER. *Lord, I unite myself today with all my brothers and sisters in this great pro-life cause.*

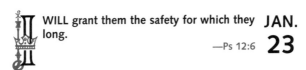

WILL grant them the safety for which they long. **JAN. 23**

—Ps 12:6

REFLECTION. Dr. Alveda King, niece of Martin Luther King, Jr., while marching at the annual March for Life was asked, "Does this remind you of the civil rights movement and the marches with your uncle?" Her response was, "This is the civil rights movement."

The message of Martin Luther King was not just about the equality of our black brothers and sisters; it was about the equality of all our brothers and sisters. Civil rights begin with the right to life.

PRAYER. *Defend Your people, O God, and protect the rights You have given to them all.*

ESUS beckoned a child to come to Him, placed it in their midst, and said, "Amen, I say to you, unless you change and become like little children, you will never enter the kingdom of heaven." **JAN. 24**

—Mt 18:2-3

REFLECTION. It is an understatement to say that children are loved by God or important to Him.

They are central, and they exemplify certain virtues and attitudes God wants us all to have.

PRAYER. *Holy Spirit, keep our minds and hearts focused on children, that we may learn from them.*

AUL, Saul, why are you persecuting Me?

—Acts 9:4

JAN. 25

REFLECTION. January 25, the Feast of the Conversion of St. Paul, concludes the Week of Prayer for Christian Unity.

Christian Unity is not about pretending that there are no differences between denominations, but rather it is about recognizing and building on what we hold in common. The pro-life movement continues to be one of the most powerful ways that Christians are coming together.

PRAYER. *Lord, we praise You for the conversions taking place each day. Bring the world to unity in You.* _____

 DO ask You to protect them from the evil one.

—Jn 17:15

JAN. 26

REFLECTION. If you are wrong on abortion, *you can't be right* on other issues.

To permit abortion, but then to cry out for the right to work, housing, education, and health care, is to say that these rights belong to *some* people but not to *all*. They obviously do not belong to those who were snuffed out by abortion.

PRAYER. *Lord, protect Your people in all of their rights, and help us to protect one another.*

HO gave man his mouth? Who makes him deaf or mute? Who gives him sight or makes him blind? Is it not I, the Lord?

—Ex 4:11

REFLECTION. God does not make mistakes. When a human being is alive, it is because God wants him or her to be alive.

People do not have to measure up to our standards or expectations in order to have dignity and deserve protection.

PRAYER. *Lord, I pray for all those who are disabled, frail, and ill. Give them Your strength and peace, and give us the eyes to see their dignity and value.* _____

 IFE, particularly human life, is the possession of God alone: therefore, one who attacks human life, in some way lifts his hand against God Himself.

—*The Gospel of Life*, 9

REFLECTION. No human being can own another, not even one's own child. God entrusts us to the care of one another, but He alone remains the owner of human life.

That's why we cannot throw a life away, no matter how small, frail, or inconvenient it may sometimes be.

PRAYER. *Lord, may all people acknowledge You as the only master of human life. May those who defend life understand that they are not only defending their brothers and sisters, but are also defending You!*

DEAR children, keep away from idols.

—1 Jn 5:21

REFLECTION. Ginette Paris wrote a book called "The Sacrament of Abortion." She claims that abortion is a sacred ritual sacrifice to the goddess Artemis.

As patroness of animals and of hunters, Artemis represents the ability to both protect and kill. The so-called right to abortion means that the mother can give either life or death to her child.

PRAYER. *Lord, free Your people from the deception of idolatry, witchcraft, and false worship. Preserve us in true worship and effective justice.*

ON seeing what had taken place, the Centurion praised God and said, "Surely, this man was innocent."

—Lk 23:47

REFLECTION. When Jesus died on the Cross, the Centurion repented for his part.

Many who used to perform abortions have now also repented, and they say, "Surely, these were innocent lives, and we are sorry." They have formed a group called the Society of Centurions. They seek God's healing and invite other abortionists to stop the killing.

PRAYER. *Lord, I pray today for the Centurions. Help them to find Your healing and peace.*

REMEMBER, of these parents you were born; what can you give them for all they gave you? —Sir 7:28

JAN. 31

REFLECTION. Some fathers are now beginning to claim the same kind of "right" to walk away from their parental responsibilities as mothers are able to do by abortion. They ask, if we can't force the mother to be a mother, why should we force the father to be a father?

The bitter fruits of Roe v. Wade continue to unfold.

PRAYER. *Lord, instill in all fathers and mothers a deep sense of responsibility for their children, born and unborn.*

WHERE the Spirit of the Lord is, there is freedom.

—2 Cor 3:17

FEB. 1

REFLECTION. A teenager in Oregon went to a legal clinic for an abortion. When she tried to leave a waiting room in order to get more information about the procedure, she found that the door to the room was locked from the outside!

She never got her questions answered, nor was she told about the risks of abortion. She sued the clinic and won.

PRAYER. *Lord, the spirit of abortion is a spirit of slavery. Let Your freedom shine forth, bringing truth, strength to do what is right, and the triumph of life.*

B E fruitful and increase in number.

—Gen 1:28

REFLECTION. God Himself is fruitful. Love always overflows into life. By commanding us as a human family to be fruitful, God is commanding us to be like Him.

He wants us to share the joy He has of giving new life. God's Word counts fertility as a great blessing and sign of His favor.

PRAYER. *Lord, thank You for the gift of fertility. Help those who are trying to conceive. Give them the blessing and joy of new life.*

H E will judge the world with justice and the nations with equity.

—Ps 96:13

REFLECTION. Some abortion advocates oppose "litmus tests" for judges. But if a judge had written an opinion about why women should not have the right to vote, wouldn't that be enough to disqualify him from being confirmed?

The fact is that we use litmus tests all the time, because certain lines should never be crossed. The killing of children by abortion is one of them.

PRAYER. *Lord, Judge of all, give wisdom to those entrusted with the task of human judgment, and let those who select them be guided by Your righteousness.*

DO not understand my own actions. For I do not do what I want; rather, I do what I hate. —Rom 7:15

FEB. 4

REFLECTION. Abortion advocates say we should "trust" women to make their own decisions. Are we then to simply trust that people won't lie, cheat, run red lights, or rob a local store?

At times, people do not respect the rights of others. That's why laws exist.

PRAYER. *Lord, with St. Paul, I acknowledge that I am inclined to sin despite my best intentions. Help us as we struggle against evil.*

 E are all His children. —Acts 17:28

FEB. 5

REFLECTION. Abortion has killed children who may have been great scientists, doctors, and inventors. Yet every life taken by abortion is equally valuable.

People do not derive their value from how productive or famous they are. The most obscure and humble life has as much intrinsic value, and as many human rights, as the most notable personalities in history.

PRAYER. *Lord, I cannot begin to imagine the plans You had for each aborted child. May we realize more deeply the value of each one of them, even the most humble and forgotten.*

ORD, open my lips. . . .

—Ps 51:17

FEB.
6

REFLECTION. If you were stranded on a desert island, and had pen, paper, and a bottle, the note you could write and put in that bottle could save your life. Before sealing it and throwing it in the sea, you would make sure that you put your very best effort behind what you said.

So it is with conversations you have about abortion. Some day they may save a life. Conduct them well.

PRAYER. *Give me confidence, O Lord, at every moment in which I will need to speak on this topic. Open my lips, that I may save lives.*

HEY sow the wind and reap the whirl-wind.

—Hos 8:7

FEB.
7

REFLECTION. There is not a single social problem that abortion has solved; every problem its advocates once said it would solve is worse today than on the day abortion became legal.

Tens of millions of children have been aborted in America since 1973. How many more have to be killed before we realize that abortion doesn't fix society's ills?

PRAYER. *Lord, save us from false hopes and deceptive remedies. Only in the paths You point out for us can we find wholeness and salvation.*

FROM my mother's womb, You have been my God.

—Ps 22:11

FEB.
8

REFLECTION. Abortion supporters sometimes ask, "Why don't you focus on caring for people who are already alive?"

When we speak about unborn children, we are not speaking about "possible" children; we are speaking about real children who are already quite alive.

PRAYER. *Father, open our eyes to recognize our brothers and sisters in their mothers' womb. Open our hearts to love them as You do.*

INDEED, everyone is "his brother's keeper," for God has committed human beings to each other's care. —*The Gospel of Life*, 19

FEB.
9

REFLECTION. Some people think that because men cannot get pregnant, they have no right to say anything about abortion.

But any human being, male or female, has the right and duty to speak up when someone's life is in danger, and do something to defend these children.

PRAYER . *Lord, thank You for entrusting me to my brothers and sisters in the human family, and for entrusting them to me. Keep us all faithful to this call.*

HATEVER authorities exist have been instituted by God.

—Rom 13:1

FEB.

10

REFLECTION. Some people say that the solution to the abortion problem is to change people's hearts. In fact, changing people's hearts is the solution to every problem that the world faces.

But that doesn't mean that we don't have laws. So long as there are people around whose hearts are not in the right place, there have to be laws to restrain their heartless activities.

PRAYER. *Father, I thank You today for laws and for lawmakers. As You guide and convert our hearts, make them also obedient to authority, and make authority obedient to Your law.*

 ORD, by now there will be a stench, for he has been dead for four days.

—Jn 11:39

FEB.

11

REFLECTION. Jesus was about to raise Lazarus, but Martha was worried about the stench. We too fear the stench. Politicians fear who will vote against them; businesses fear who will stop supporting them.

"Surely, there will be a stench." And that becomes the excuse not to act—even when we know that Jesus has authority over death.

PRAYER. *Lord, free us from our fears and calculations, and make us bold as we battle the culture of death.*

YOU have come to Jesus . . . and to the sprinkled blood that speaks more powerfully than even the blood of Abel. —Heb 12:24

FEB. 12

REFLECTION. In the culture of death, the blood of tens of millions of unborn children is shed together with that of Jesus. Scripture teaches that the blood of the innocent cries out to God.

Fortunately, it also teaches that the blood of Jesus cries out louder, calling for mercy, forgiveness, and reconciliation.

PRAYER. *Lord, in Communion we receive Your Body and Blood. May we weep for the blood of the babies; may we be consoled as we receive the Blood of Christ.*

THIS is how we know what love is: He laid down His life for us. —1 Jn 3:16

FEB. 13

REFLECTION. The word "love" is the most misused, abused, and confused word in the English language. We say: I love ice cream, I love my mother, I love my wife, I love God. And some use "love" to justify abortion.

The real meaning of love is found at the Cross. Love says, "I sacrifice myself for the good of the other person." Abortion says, "I sacrifice the other person for the good of myself."

PRAYER. *Lord, I commit myself today to the love of others, especially those most in need.*

GREET one another with a holy kiss.

—Rom 16:16

REFLECTION. On Valentine's Day, many messages of affection are exchanged.

A culture of life avoids two extremes—one, which looks down on all affection and thinks that the only good things are the things of the spirit; and the other, which allows the emotions to run out of control, with no discipline.

PRAYER. *Holy Spirit, font of love both human and divine, bless us today with understanding, balance, and grace. Enable us to devote ourselves to the service of God and neighbor.*

DO not show partiality in judging; hear both small and great alike.

—Deut 1:17

FEB. **15**

REFLECTION. Some say an embryo is too small to have human rights. But rights do not depend on size.

Do men have more rights than women because they are generally larger? Are shorter people to enjoy fewer protections than tall people? The size of a person has nothing to do with his or her value.

PRAYER. *O God, You have dominion over all things great and small, and have created a vast variety of life. May we reverence the very smallest of our brothers and sisters.*

THE foundation of these principles cannot be temporary and ever-changing "majority opinions." **FEB.** **16**
—*The Gospel of Life,* 70

REFLECTION. Abortion supporters often say most Americans are pro-choice.

But the pro-choice position is that a person can choose an abortion any time in pregnancy, for any reason, and even at taxpayer's expense. This position has never been embraced by a majority of Americans, and never will be.

PRAYER. *Father, send Your Spirit upon Your people to help us discern the law written on our hearts. Protect us from falling into false and harmful opinions.*

THE Lord said to Cain, "Where is your brother Abel?" "I don't know," he replied. **FEB.** **17**
—Gen 4:9

REFLECTION. In 1973 the Supreme Court was asked the same question posed to Cain and gave the same answer.

Unable to admit that unborn children are our brothers and sisters, the Supreme Court said, "We need not resolve the difficult question of when human life begins . . . the judiciary . . . is not competent to speculate as to the answer." That's the same as "I don't know."

PRAYER. *Lord, may all of us recognize and love our brothers and sisters, born and unborn.*

HOEVER addresses his brother in an insulting way will answer for it before the Sanhedrin, and whoever calls his brother a fool will be liable to the fires of Gehenna.

FEB.
18

—Mt 5:22

REFLECTION. Jesus says that using dehumanizing language is sinful.

Throughout history, groups that have been oppressed—like slaves and Holocaust victims—have first been called names. It also happens to the unborn, who have been called "parasites," "tissue," and "medical waste."

PRAYER. *Lord, may we affirm one another, including the unborn, with language that inspires respect and love.*

 ON of man, can these bones live? I said, "O Sovereign LORD, You alone know." Then He said to me, "Prophesy to these bones."

FEB.
19

—Ezek 37:3-4

REFLECTION. When God commanded Ezekiel to preach to the bones, he had a choice between doing the foolish thing or the dangerous thing (disobeying God). Ezekiel chose to preach to the bones, and they came to life.

We are in the same dilemma. Some will say it's impossible to end abortion. But we dare not distrust or disobey God. We will preach to the bones.

PRAYER. *Lord, may I trust the power of Your word to bring a culture of death back to life.*

ITH the help of the Lord I have brought forth a man.

—Gen 4:1

REFLECTION. This was the declaration of Eve upon becoming the first mother. The *help of the Lord* is essential, for He alone has dominion over human life and is its origin. Parents cooperate with God in bringing forth life, but are not its owners or ultimate source.

Because this whole process is under God's dominion, we are not permitted to interrupt it.

PRAYER. *Lord, I pray today for all parents. May they recognize the awesome privilege they have to cooperate with You in bringing forth new life. I pray in Jesus' name.*

ORDS cannot escape the reality of things: procured abortion is the direct and deliberate killing of a human being.

—*The Gospel of Life, 58*

REFLECTION. In discussing abortion, its supporters never defend the act of abortion itself, but only the alleged right of someone to have one. They focus on the freedom to choose it, but avoid describing what is chosen.

Our job is to focus the discussion on abortion itself, on what the act is.

PRAYER. *Come, Holy Spirit of truth. Give us grace to always face truth honestly, and enable us to challenge those who would evade it.*

THE defense and promotion of human life are not the monopoly of anyone, but rather the responsibility and task of all. —*The Gospel of Life*, 91

FEB. 22

REFLECTION. In *The Gospel of Life*, Pope John Paul states that no person or group, including the Catholic Church, has a monopoly on the defense of life. He called on all Christians, and all people of goodwill, to cooperate with each other in this effort.

Indeed, we all need one another to accomplish the works of justice.

PRAYER. *Lord, enable those who work for the defense of life to accept one another and to rejoice in the fruits of their collaboration.*

YOU saw me in the womb . . . —Ps 139:15

FEB. 23

REFLECTION. Some people think that embryos are too small to be persons with rights.

But from the perspective of our faith, we can ask a similar question about the Eucharist. The smallest particle is the Body of Christ. Is the host too small to be worshiped and adored as our Lord and God?

PRAYER. *Lord, help us to realize that value does not depend on size. May our Eucharistic faith lead us to serve the most vulnerable.*

THE question "Where does one begin?" is easy to answer: "We must begin with a commitment never to intentionally kill, or collude in the killing, of any innocent human life." —US Bishops' Pastoral Plan for Pro-life Activities, 2001

FEB. 24

REFLECTION. There is a big difference between abortion on the one hand, and war and capital punishment on the other.

War and capital punishment, when justified, are in their essence carried out for the defense of life; abortion is in its essence the destruction of life.

PRAYER. *Lord, give wisdom to Your people, that they may properly exercise their responsibility to defend life in every circumstance.*

HE will turn the hearts of the fathers to their children . . . —Mal 3:24

FEB. 25

REFLECTION. Though men cannot *have* abortions, they can *choose* abortions. A sin is committed when somebody willingly and knowingly chooses a moral wrong.

If, then, a man suggests or pressures his partner to have an abortion, he has committed the sin of abortion.

PRAYER. *Lord, You are the source of all fatherhood. Bless all men with the wisdom to protect their children born and unborn.*

MEN, I say to you, there are some standing here who will not taste death before they see that the kingdom of God has come with power. —Mk 9:1

FEB. 26

REFLECTION. The second coming has not happened yet, so what did Jesus mean? He meant that they would see Him in the glory of the Resurrection.

He appeared to many of the disciples after His Resurrection and told them full authority had been given to Him. These disciples saw the kingdom of God established in power and glory.

PRAYER. *Lord Jesus, You rule the universe. May we find the freedom that comes from subjecting all our choices to You.*

 OU created my inmost being; You knit me together in my mother's womb. I praise You because I am wonderfully made; awesome are Your works.

FEB. 27

—Ps 139:13-14

REFLECTION. This psalm not only declares that God made us in the womb, but also that the life in the womb belongs completely to Him, is called by Him, and is destined to fulfill a plan given only to that individual from all eternity.

PRAYER. *Lord, forgive those who deny the child's right to live thereby destroying Your loving plan initiated from all eternity.*

HOEVER humbles himself and becomes like this child is the greatest in the kingdom of heaven. —Mt 18:4

REFLECTION. There is a natural humility about children that God wants us to imitate. They know they are smaller and weaker and in need of protection and provision. God wants us to know our dependence on Him in the same way.

The dependence of children, therefore, is meant to evoke from us the same kind of care that God gives us all.

PRAYER. *Lord, thank You for the example of children. May their dependence move the hearts of those around them to love, protect, and care for them in every circumstance.*

THE boy is to be a Nazirite, set apart to God from birth. —Jdg 13:7

FEB. **29**

REFLECTION. The Angel of the Lord tells Samson's parents that his special relationship with God is set before his birth.

God's special relationship with the child in the womb appears regularly in Scripture, highlighting the sanctity of the lives of all such children.

PRAYER. *Lord, we cannot know the plans You have for each unborn child. May all people respect the special call given to each of us.*

36

RUE "compassion" brings one to share the suffering of the other, not to eliminate the one whose suffering he cannot tolerate. —*The Gospel of Life*, 66

REFLECTION. The word "compassion" comes from the Latin words meaning "to suffer with." Love brings us closer to people, and when they are in pain, love wants to come closer still. Love gladly suffers for and with the one who is loved.

The so-called "right to die" is really a clever disguise for the right to kill.

PRAYER. *Lord, free us from the selfishness that wants to run away from the suffering of others. Instead, fill us with true compassion so that we may suffer with them.*

 ESCUE those being led away to death; hold back those staggering toward slaughter. —Prov 24:11

REFLECTION. Many think that another person's abortion, though wrong, is none of their business. But whenever someone's choice destroys someone else's life, that's everyone's business.

God makes it our business by commanding us to rescue those in danger. God makes it our business because He entrusts us to the care of one another. Ours is the business of love.

PRAYER. *Lord, I pray today for all those whose lives are in danger. They are my brothers and sisters. Strengthen me to intervene for them.*

YOU shall not murder.

—Ex 20:13

REFLECTION. God's own finger wrote in stone the commandments He gave to Moses, and through Moses to us.

"You shall not murder" refers to the deliberate act of taking an innocent human life, and is forever prohibited precisely because all life belongs to God, and God is life itself.

PRAYER. *Lord, Your prohibition on murder was literally written in stone and is as unchangeable as You are. Give all Your people the gift of obedience.*

BLESSED are those who mourn, for they will be comforted.

—Mt 5:4

REFLECTION. We are blessed, indeed, if we mourn over our sins and over the evils in the world, like the daily killing of children by abortion.

When is the last time we shed tears over the shedding of blood, and wept for the lives of these babies killed and moms and dads wounded? Let us pray for the gift of those tears!

PRAYER. *Lord, give me a broken heart over abortion. Give me the grace to do my part in ending this evil, and give me comfort, as You bring justice to the earth.*

F men who are fighting hit a pregnant woman and she gives birth prematurely, but there is no serious injury, the offender must be fined. . . . But if there is serious injury, you are to take life for life, eye for eye.

MAR.

5

—Ex 21: 22-24

REFLECTION. The phrase, "no serious injury" applies equally to mother and child. According to Hebrew scholar Dr. Gleason Archer, "There is no second class status attached to the fetus under this rule. The fetus is just as valuable as the mother."

PRAYER. *Lord, as You care for every one of Your children, may we do likewise.*

 ANNAH wept much and prayed to the Lord . . . "Remember me, and not forget your servant but give her a son . . ."

MAR.

6

—1 Sam 1:10-11

REFLECTION. The people of the Old Testament regarded barrenness as a curse, a source of great shame and sorrow. Fertility, on the other hand, was a blessing and a sign of God's favor.

Many people who suffer from infertility are very close and faithful to God. The attitude of a culture that aborts children, however, increases their anguish all the more.

PRAYER. *Lord, may we again see children as a blessing. Give that blessing to all who long for a child.*

ITH glory and honor You crowned him, giving him power over the works of Your hands. —Ps 8:5-7

MAR. 7

REFLECTION. Here is the key in the battle for life. Not only did God make us, but He values us, crowning us with dominion over the rest of creation.

The Bible tells us of a God who is madly in love with us, so much so that He became one of us and even died for us while we were still offending Him.

PRAYER. *Lord, we are amazed at Your love for us. May we learn from it and imitate it, as we love and protect one another.*

 AN a mother forget the baby at her breast and have no compassion on the child she has borne? Though she may forget, I will not forget you! —Isa 49:15

MAR. 8

REFLECTION. In assuring His people of His unfailing love for them, God seeks an extreme example to make His point: He speaks of the bond between a mother and the child of her womb. He declares that the breaking of that bond is practically unthinkable to Him.

PRAYER. *Lord, You have established the bond between mother and child and used it as an example of the most faithful commitment. Strengthen all mothers and protect all their children.*

EPENT, and believe in the Gospel.

—Mk 1:15

REFLECTION. At the start of Lent, we receive the ashes that remind us of the power of sin and death, which return us to dust. Yet we wear the ashes in the form of a cross, professing that Christ has conquered death and restored life.

Lent prepares us to share the victory of Life and to live as the People of Life!

PRAYER. *Father, I repent of all my sins. Turn me away from death and toward life so that I may find freedom in Jesus the Lord.*

 OME people slanderously accuse us of proposing, "Let us do evil so that good may result." —Rom 3:8

REFLECTION. When we do choose evil, not only does that have consequences *on the outside,* but it changes us on the inside as well. The same is true when we do good.

The battle for life is one that we conduct only by choosing good. We can never destroy or kill in the name of life.

PRAYER. *Lord, how deep is the darkness and how great the chaos when we think that the end justifies the means. Protect us from trying to justify evil for good intentions.*

TURN away from sin and be faithful to the Gospel.

—Liturgy of Ash Wednesday

MAR.
11

REFLECTION. Lent is the time when we learn more deeply why we are pro-life. Turning away from sin means we put God above our "freedom of choice."

Believing in the Gospel means we believe in life and reject the forces of death, including abortion.

PRAYER. *Lord, I fully repent of all the times I have given my choices more weight than Yours. This Lent, renew my fidelity to You. May I be a living example of what it means to choose life.*

THEY mutilated their sons and daughters by fire . . . till the Lord, in His great anger against Israel, put them away out of His sight. —2 Kgs 17:17-18

MAR.
12

REFLECTION. The people of God inherited the Holy Land according to God's promise but then offended Him. Therefore, the Assyrians swept through the land and brought them into exile.

The shedding of innocent blood by child-sacrifice was one of the major reasons that this occurred.

PRAYER. *Lord, You taught Your people that their destiny on the land depended upon their fidelity to Your covenant. Keep us faithful in our day and free of the guilt of child sacrifice.*

WE prepare to celebrate the Paschal Mystery with mind and heart renewed.

MAR. 13

—*Sacramentary*, Preface of Lent 1

REFLECTION. Lent is a season in which we prepare to celebrate Christ's total victory over death and our share in His life by baptism. Death was not part of God's original plan for us.

Standing with Christ in His new life means standing against whatever destroys life.

PRAYER. *Lord, in this Lenten season, strengthen and renew our commitment to be the People of Life.*

ANYONE who wishes to follow Me must deny himself. . . .

MAR. 14

—Mt 16:24

REFLECTION. The traditional practice of "giving something up for Lent" is a practice of self-denial. It means we say no to ourselves and yes to God and others.

This reverses the pattern of sin, particularly abortion, which says yes to ourselves and no to God and others.

PRAYER. *Lord, as I practice self-denial, I offer my sacrifices for children. May we say yes to You and yes to the unborn.*

IF we endure, we shall also reign with Him. **MAR.**

—2 Tim 2:12 **15**

REFLECTION. In Lent, the Church enters more deeply into meditation on the suffering, death, and Resurrection of the Lord Jesus.

Life was sacred because He made it, and by His Passion and Resurrection it is even more sacred because it is now raised to the heights of heaven to reign with Him.

PRAYER. *Lord, I am filled with wonder at Your love for human life, everyone, born and unborn! May our laws and practices treat humans with the highest respect due them.*

———————

WALK in love, as Christ loved us and **MAR.** gave Himself up for us.

—Eph 5:2 **16**

REFLECTION. Jesus endured crucifixion out of love for us, giving Himself away that we might have life. Abortion, on the other hand, is the opposite of love because it takes life.

Love says, "I sacrifice myself for the good of the other person." Abortion says, "I sacrifice the other person for the good of myself."

PRAYER. *Father, fill me and all people with the same love by which Your Son gave Himself away on the Cross. Grant that we may sacrifice ourselves and never sacrifice others.*

F anyone is rich in worldly possessions and sees a brother in need but refuses to open his heart, how can the love of God abide in him?

MAR. 17

—1 Jn 3:17

REFLECTION. Our relationship with God depends on how well we tend to the needs of others. If this applies to the need others have for material possessions, how much more does it apply to the need others have for life itself?

God's love cannot survive in us if we turn our backs on the unborn and all whose lives are in danger.

PRAYER. *Abide with us, Lord, so that we may see those in need and open our hearts to them.*

 Y righteous servant will justify many and He will bear their iniquities.

MAR. 18

—Isa 53:11

REFLECTION. Lent is a season of life. The Passion, death, and Resurrection of Christ have brought us the new life we now live.

We commit ourselves to join all our suffering to His for our own salvation and that of the whole world.

PRAYER. *Jesus, I offer You all my sufferings, that they may be borne in union with Your Cross and may help bring about a Culture of Life starting in me.*

RISE, take the child and His mother, and flee to Egypt. **MAR. 19**

—Mt 2:13

REFLECTION. St. Joseph is a model for all fathers in his example of faithfulness and protection of his family.

Thousands of times a day, children are aborted because of the choice of a father, who fails to show that faithfulness and willingness to protect the child he has helped conceive.

PRAYER. *Lord, bless all fathers so that they may welcome every child and join the child's mother in saying yes to life.*

———

 AND so Pilate, . . . handed Him over to be crucified. **MAR. 20**

—Mk 15:15

REFLECTION. The Passion of Christ was far more horrible than our crucifixes portray. He suffered to rescue the human life He had created, to snatch it from the kingdom of death and bring it into His kingdom of life.

Let us remember this Lent that Jesus endured His Passion for every unborn child in the womb. He endured every pain that the unborn might be saved as well as the born.

PRAYER. *Lord, lessen my fear and increase my courage, that I may suffer with You for the sake of life.*

HOEVER receives one such child in My name receives Me.

—Mt 18:5

REFLECTION. How do we welcome Jesus? His answer is, by receiving a child. The Lord identifies Himself with the helplessness of a child and with the relationship of giving that a child brings forth.

The first "receiving" of the child is from the parents, but it does not stop there. We are all called to "receive" every child who is conceived.

PRAYER. *Lord, as You bring forth new life each day into our world, bring it forth also in our hearts, and enable us to receive every life, knowing that thereby we receive You.*

O you reject Satan? And all his empty promises?

—*Sacramentary*, Renewal of Baptismal Promises

REFLECTION. Lent is a time to pray for the catechumens of the Church who are preparing to be baptized at the Easter Vigil. The rest of us will renew our Baptismal Promises. In these vows, we reject the empty promises of the devil.

One of those empty promises is abortion.

PRAYER. *Thank You, Lord, for the power of baptism in my life by which I am able to affirm life each day against the power of death!*

EVEN now, I know that God will grant you whatever you ask of Him.
—Jn 11:22

MAR. 23

REFLECTION. Lazarus was in the tomb four days, but Martha and Mary expressed to Jesus the hope that He could raise him. Even now.

That should be our theme as we fight the evil of abortion. Some will say it has gone on so long it cannot be changed. But despite the culture of death, we are called to hope in the God Who has not changed and in His power to defeat abortion. Even now.

PRAYER. *Lord, we are people of hope. Grant us perseverance and victory in the battle for life.*

BEFORE I formed you in the womb I knew you, before you were born I set you apart; I appointed you as a prophet to the nations.
—Jer 1:5

MAR. 24

REFLECTION. These verses show us that God not only recognizes the unborn child but also enters into a relationship with that child, bestowing on him or her a unique vocation.

This affirms the personhood of unborn children and motivates us to work for their protection.

PRAYER. *Lord, give all the children in the womb the opportunity to fulfill the vocation You have given to each one of them.*

ET it be done to me according to Your word. **MAR. 25**

—Lk 1:38

REFLECTION. The *truth* of God's Word exists before Mary's own choosing. She submits to a word, a truth she did not create.

At the heart of the "pro-choice" mentality is the idea that *we create our own truth.* This mentality holds that the value of the unborn child, and that child's right to exist, *depend upon* the choice of the mother.

PRAYER. *Lord, let it be done to me also according to Your word, now and always!*

HE LORD God formed the man from the dust of the ground and breathed into his nostrils the breath of life, and the man became a living being. **MAR. 26**

—Gen 2:7

REFLECTION. The act of creation described in Genesis 2:7 is a sovereign act. God did not have to do it.

Yet without our asking for it or earning it, God brought us out of nothingness and into life, and sustains our existence at every moment.

PRAYER. *Lord, teach us the lesson that there is no God but You and that no human being has dominion over life. Fill us with awe in Your presence.*

WHEN I am lifted up from the earth, I will draw all to Myself.

—Jn 12:32

MAR. 27

REFLECTION. Jesus fulfills this promise in the Eucharist, which builds up the Church. All those receiving Communion today receive the very same Jesus.

God, enthroned in heaven, is drawing all these people to Himself and also to one another. We become one body and are responsible to foster the unity of the entire human family.

PRAYER. *Lord, continue to fulfill Your promise of unity. Free us from the divisions that result from aborting children and killing the sick. May we build a culture of life!*

IN everything, deal with others as you would like them to deal with you.

—Mt 7:12

MAR. 28

REFLECTION. The "Golden Rule" applies also when the "others" are unborn children scheduled for abortion. We are to do what we would want others to do if we were in danger.

We can stop wondering how many people we should risk offending, or how many positions we should risk losing. "In everything, do to others what you would have them do to you."

PRAYER. *Father, in this simple rule, You have shown us how far we need to go in defending human lives. Give us the courage to carry it out.*

COME to Me, all you who are weary and overburdened, and I will give you rest.
—Mt 11:28

REFLECTION. The burden Jesus is talking about is not just that you have bills to pay, tasks to accomplish, or a busy schedule to keep.

He is speaking about the burden we feel when we see the rights of our brothers and sisters ignored and innocent blood shed. He is speaking of the work we do to correct these injustices and build a culture of life.

PRAYER. *Thank You, Lord, for refreshing me each day in the battle for life!*

LOVE your neighbor as yourself. I am the LORD.
—Lev 19:18

REFLECTION. The command "Love your neighbor" does not have distinctions, limitations, or exclusions. It includes our unborn neighbors.

And to love them "as yourself" does not simply mean to love them "to the degree" that you love yourself; it means first to recognize them as a person like yourself.

PRAYER. *Let Your command of love, O Lord, free us all from the prejudices that distract us. Open our eyes to see every human person as our neighbor and to act accordingly.*

THERE is reason for you to rejoice, even if now for a little while you must suffer trials of many kinds. —1 Pet 1:6

MAR.
31

REFLECTION. Today is "Terri's Day," the anniversary of the death of Terri Schiavo who was killed by deliberate dehydration.

Some say, "I wouldn't want to live like *that*." We would not want to live like the homeless, or those with various forms of addiction or severe financial crises. But like all God's children, we respect their right to life.

PRAYER. *Give continued consolation, Lord, to Terri's family, and protection to the vulnerable.*

" **I**F you wish to enter into life, keep the commandments." He said, "Which ones?" And Jesus answered, "You shall not kill. . . . "
—Mt 19:17-18

APR.
1

REFLECTION. The prohibition of murder is mentioned first by Jesus when He refers to the commandments in answer to the rich young man's question about how to reach eternal life.

Taking one's neighbor's life is the most direct contradiction to the love of that neighbor and to the blessing God wants us to enjoy, the foundation of which is life.

PRAYER. *Lord, all the good You give us depends on life. Bring an end to all killing so that we may each walk the path to life eternal.*

RULERS are a source of fear not to those who do good but rather to those who do evil. **APR. 2**
—Rom 13:3

REFLECTION. There is a big difference between abortion on the one hand, and war and capital punishment on the other.

War and capital punishment, when justified, are carried out by the authority of the state to restrain those guilty of doing harm; abortion is always carried out by the authority of an individual to destroy one completely innocent of doing any harm.

PRAYER. *Protect Your people from all harm, O Lord, and give Your strength to those You have appointed to preserve our peace and security.*

 WHEN Elizabeth heard Mary's greeting, the baby leaped in her womb. **APR. 3**
—Lk 1:41

REFLECTION. Scripture uses the word "brephos" for the unborn as it does for other children (Lk 18:15, Acts 7:19, 1 Pet 2:2).

Luke's Gospel uses the word "baby" or "child" (Gr. *brephos*) to describe John the Baptist prior to his birth. But one chapter later (2:12,16), the already born Christ child is also referred to as a "baby" (*brephos*).

PRAYER. *Lord, Your word speaks of the born and the unborn in the same terms. Give us the same respect and love for both.*

This gate lay a poor man named Lazarus, covered with sores.

—Lk 16:20

APR.
4

REFLECTION. Lazarus got nothing when he
begged at the rich man's door. The rich man
thought that because Lazarus had less, he was
worth less. He failed to recognize the one in
need as his brother.

In our time there are many who fail to recognize that the unborn child is their brother, their
sister, the Lazarus of the 21st century.

PRAYER. *Lord, use our riches for the lowliest
among us. May none of us repeat the rich man's
mistake.*

———————

GOD is faithful, and He will not allow
you to be tried beyond your strength.
But together with the trial He will also
provide a way out and the strength to
bear it.

—1 Cor 10:13

APR.
5

REFLECTION. Those who have abortions do not
have them because of "freedom of choice," but
rather because they feel they have *no freedom*
and *no choice*. Mountains of pressure and con-
fusion fall upon them.

Yet in the struggle against temptation and sin,
God always provides the way to say no to evil
and yes to good.

PRAYER. *Lord, bless all those who counsel others against abortion. May they effectively
announce the power of Your grace.*

AM the way, and the truth, and the life.

—Jn 14:6

APR.
6

REFLECTION. Jesus is the Way precisely because He is Truth and Life. "The Son of God came into the world to destroy the works of the devil" (1 Jn 3:8), and as John 8 reveals, those works are lies and murder.

Jesus, the Way, overcomes those works precisely by being the Truth (undoing the devil's lies) and the Life (undoing the devil's works of death.)

PRAYER. *Lord, we thirst for Your Truth; we embrace Your Life; we cling to You. You are the Way to our eternal salvation.*

 F you were blind, you would have no guilt; but since you claim, "We see," your guilt remains.

—Jn 9:41

APR.
7

REFLECTION. The Pharisees simply refused to accept the evidence of the miracle of Jesus healing the man born blind. Not to know the truth is not a sin. But the refusal to know is.

Some refuse to face the truth about the child in the womb and the violence of abortion. The sin is not in blindness, but in the refusal to see.

PRAYER. *Lord, we want to see. Preserve us from the guilt of choosing to be blind. Help us to choose life!*

ASK the Lord of the harvest to send forth laborers for His harvest.

—Mt 9:38

APR. 8

REFLECTION. The future of the priesthood is in the seminarians of today. Their training needs to make them strong and effective pro-life advocates.

In fact, many of these young men have found their vocation precisely through the pro-life movement.

PRAYER. *Lord, let Your call be heard by those whom You want to be priests, and make them strong yet gentle heralds of the Gospel of Life!*

DO not put an innocent or honest person to death, for I will not acquit the guilty.

—Ex 23:7

APR. 9

REFLECTION. The shedding of innocent blood was strictly forbidden to the people of the Covenant.

The giving of the law and the establishment of the way of life they were to live in the Promised Land set them apart from other nations who did not know the true God, and as a result, did not have the same respect for human life.

PRAYER. *Lord, we are blessed to know You, the God of Life. Keep us faithful to Your covenant and immersed in the awareness of how sacred every life is.*

GOD'S love was revealed to us in this way: God sent His only-begotten Son into the world so that we might have life through Him. —1 Jn 4:9

APR.
10

REFLECTION. The bible teaches us that God is love, and it likewise teaches us that this love leads to life.

Love always gives life; it never takes it. That's why Christians are pro-life.

PRAYER. *Father, thank You for revealing Your love in Christ, Who is life and gives life. May we be immersed in that love so that we too may always be defenders of life.*

THE LORD God took the man and put him in the Garden of Eden to work it and take care of it. —Gen 2:15

APR.
11

REFLECTION. The Lord commands Adam to care for the garden. But Adam failed, because he did not exercise the necessary vigilance to prevent the serpent from entering and then tempting Eve.

A key reason why women get abortions is the failure of the baby's father to encourage them to do what is right.

PRAYER. *Lord, send Your Spirit upon all men. May they not fail to guard and care for their families even amid the most difficult temptations against life.*

NY policy that violates the natural right to life that belongs to an innocent person is unjust and therefore is incapable of having the force of law.

APR. 12

—*The Gospel of Life, 90*

REFLECTION. The Church does not say that laws allowing abortion are just "bad laws." The Church declares that they are no laws at all.

Rather, they are acts of violence, and must be resisted rather than obeyed. To be valid and binding, a law must never contradict the law of God.

PRAYER. *Father, as we live amidst unjust laws, give us the grace to recognize them as invalid, to say so to others, and to work to change them.*

OME scribes who were Pharisees noticed that Jesus was eating with sinners and tax collectors, and they asked His disciples, "Why does He eat with tax collectors and sinners?"

APR. 13

—Mk 2:16

REFLECTION. Jesus broke down the false barriers that people set up among themselves and instead acknowledged the equal human dignity of every individual, despite what common opinion might say.

He moved toward those who needed His help, rather than rejecting them because of who they were.

PRAYER. *Holy Spirit, give us the mind of Christ that we may never cast off any human person or group of people, but rather be vehicles of Your care for them.*

TAKE care that you do not despise one of these little ones, for I tell you that their Angels in heaven gaze continually on the face of My heavenly Father.

APR. 14

—Mt 18:10

REFLECTION. All of us, including the smallest children, have Angels in heaven who worship the Father and reflect to us His care. If an Angel is assigned to guard each human life, how much more are fellow human beings called to respect them.

PRAYER. *Lord, fill us with awe and reverence for life. Though we are not able to see the Angels, remind us of their presence, too, through the face of every human person.*

WE who are many are one body, for we all partake of the one bread.

APR. 15

—1 Cor 10:17

REFLECTION. When we call each other "brothers and sisters," we are not merely using a metaphor that dimly reflects the unity between children of the same parents. Our unity in Christ is even stronger than that because we do have common blood: the Blood of Christ!

The result of the Eucharist is that we become one, and this obliges us to be as concerned for each other as we are for our own bodies.

PRAYER. *Lord, thank You for the unity which marks the Culture of Life.*

OIN in imitating me, and take note of those who conduct themselves in accord with the model you have in us. —Phil 3:17

APR. 16

REFLECTION. The US bishops have said Catholic institutions should not "give awards, honors, or platforms to those who act contrary to Church teaching on fundamental moral principles."

Honoring supporters of abortion not only contradicts Church teaching; it contradicts American ideals and basic human decency.

PRAYER. *Lord, as we strive to follow You, continue to give us good examples of fidelity, not only in the Saints but in the leaders You give us today.*

 EFUSING to participate in doing wrong is not only a moral duty but a fundamental human right.

—*The Gospel of Life, 74*

APR. 17

REFLECTION. One of the key battlegrounds in the fight for life is to defend the freedom of doctors, nurses, pharmacists, judges and other professionals to refuse to violate their conscience as they carry out their work.

At times this freedom is secure, and at other times, fidelity carries a high price.

PRAYER. *Lord, provide light and strength to all those who may face the loss of their jobs in order to maintain their integrity. Protect us all as we do what is right.*

WHAT is man that You are mindful of him, the son of man that You care for him? —Ps 8:5

APR. 18

REFLECTION. A television movie had a scene in which two women were arguing. One said, "But you don't get it, you don't get it—you just killed someone." And the other responded, "No, you don't get it—I don't care!"

Many abortion supporters know abortion kills children; they just don't care.

PRAYER. *Lord, we ask for more than education and knowledge. We ask that You fill our world with hearts that care. May those who have forgotten how to care learn from our example.*

WOMEN play a unique and decisive role, in thought and action, in the conversion of culture to be pro-life. Theirs is the task of promoting a "new feminism."

APR. 19

—*The Gospel of Life*, 99

REFLECTION. The early feminist leader Susan B. Anthony said, "Abortion is child murder."

Women are equal in dignity to men because all human beings are equal in dignity. And "all" includes the human beings still living in the womb.

PRAYER. *Lord, help us to truly understand the meaning of "equality." Free the legitimate efforts for women's advancement from the mistaken notion that this includes abortion.*

HAVE listened to everything you said to me and have set a king over you. **APR. 20**

—1 Sam 12:1

REFLECTION. When politicians neglect the unborn, they are not representing all the people. Representing the people starts with protecting them.

Yes, an elected official has to represent all the people. That means that we cannot draw artificial lines that say that some people aren't really people after all.

PRAYER. *Lord, give us leaders who will indeed represent and protect all the people.*

 ET us love not in word or speech but in deed and truth. **APR. 21**

—1 Jn 3:18

REFLECTION. There is an axiom in psychiatry that says, "Believe behavior." See what the speaker does.

The "pro-choice" movement, for all its rhetoric, leaves women alone with the pain of abortion. The pro-life movement, through thousands of pregnancy resource centers, offers women real help in their need and the gifts of life and peace.

PRAYER. *Holy Spirit, free us from a superficial commitment to goodness. Continue to turn our good words into good actions so that life may flourish.*

AND while they were in the field, Cain attacked his brother Abel and killed him.
—Gen 4:8

APR. 22

REFLECTION. The first murder in history was within the immediate family, brother killing brother. One of the reasons abortion and euthanasia are preeminent issues today is that those forms of killing likewise take place by one family member upon another.

The family is the sanctuary of life. It should be the safest place.

PRAYER. *Lord, have mercy on the families of our world. Fill them with the spirit of welcome and love, of nurture and protection.*

YOU did not choose Me. Rather, I chose you.
—Jn 15:16

APR. 23

REFLECTION. Baptism is a sacrament of welcome. God chooses us long before we choose, and all the chosen welcome each other.

This is the exact opposite of the mindset of abortion, which ignores God's choice and says that *we* can choose *not* to welcome children into the community. Let's thank God for baptism and for life!

PRAYER. *Lord, as a people made one by baptism, may we grow in the spirit of welcome and rejoice in all those You continue to add to the human family.*

OU have died, and your life is hidden with Christ in God.

—Col 3:3

APR. 24

REFLECTION. On Easter, many throughout the world are baptized into the Church, and those already baptized renew the vows of their baptism.

By baptism, we are immersed in the new life of Christ. Thanks to baptism, God looks at us through the eyes of His Son, and says, "You are My child; you died on the cross, therefore you will rise from the dead."

PRAYER. *Father, thank You for immersing me into the death and Resurrection of Your Son!*

 T dawn on the first day of the week . . . there was a violent earthquake.

—Mt 28:1-2a

APR. 25

REFLECTION. In the Old Testament, earthquakes are a sign of the coming of God, the breaking in of the new age in which God's kingdom will flourish.

That is what happens, of course, at the Resurrection. A new chapter of history now begins in which the risen life of Christ is accepted by believers and overcomes humanity's slavery to death.

PRAYER. *Father, in the light of the Resurrection, may we continue to extend Your victory over death!*

N Angel of the Lord descended from heaven, came and rolled back the stone, and sat upon it. —Mt 28:2

REFLECTION. The stone is what sealed human beings in the grave. By sitting on it, the Angel says that death is conquered—not only Jesus' death but all death.

The stone is not going to roll back; it cannot any longer hold humanity captive to the grave. Our destiny is now the heights of heaven.

PRAYER. *Lord, Your power is greater than death. May Easter give me confidence to be a witness to Life!*

VERYONE who does evil hates the light and avoids coming near the light so that his misdeeds may not be exposed.
—Jn 3:20

REFLECTION. A key priority of the pro-life movement must be to expose the corruption of the abortion industry. Making abortion legal never made it safe; keeping it legal can never keep it safe.

You can't practice vice virtuously. If you are willing to take a baby's life, you will be willing to do many other kinds of evil as well.

PRAYER. *Lord, bring into the light the evils being done behind closed doors in abortion centers so that our nation may repent and be healed in Jesus' Name.*

HEN they heard that He was alive ... they refused to believe it.

—Mk 16:11

APR.
28

REFLECTION. On Easter morning, the women who had seen the Risen Lord were greeted by disbelieving Apostles.

The Apostles clearly were not engaged in wishful thinking. They came to believe because they saw and touched the risen Lord. This gives us confidence. The victory of life is more than wishful thinking.

PRAYER. *Lord, drive the power of doubt away, and enable me to spread the certainty of the victory of life!*

HEY ran from the tomb to inform His disciples ...

—Mt 28:8

APR.
29

REFLECTION. On the morning of Jesus' Resurrection, the women having seen the empty tomb, ran back to the Disciples. Peter and John, having heard the women's story, ran toward the tomb. And in the end, of course, all the Apostles ran into the world to announce this greatest news of history.

We, too, must run to announce the Gospel of Life with vigor and to save the unborn with urgency.

PRAYER. *Lord, fill me with the vigor of Easter each day so that I may announce the victory of Life!*

HY do you look among the dead for One Who is alive? He is not here. He has been raised.

—Lk 24:5-6

REFLECTION. How easy it is for people to seek the living one among the dead. Despair causes them to look to death as a solution. But death is never a solution.

When we look to Jesus, we find the Living One, and He strengthens us to choose life.

PRAYER. *Lord, we do not seek You among the dead. Grant that Your people may never turn to death to take away their pain, but only to You, the Living Lord.*

LESSED are you among women, and blessed is the fruit of your womb.

MAY 1

—Lk 1:42

REFLECTION. May is marked by the beautiful ceremony of the May crowning. We present to Mary, the mother of Life, bouquets of flowers that represent life.

By doing this, we honor Mary for saying yes to the Life of God in her womb.

PRAYER. *Mary, we ask you today to intercede for all those who find it difficult to accept the gift of new life, whether within their own womb or in someone else. Help them say Yes.*

HO will roll back the stone for us from the entrance to the tomb?

MAY 2

—Mk 16:3

REFLECTION. On Easter morning, little did the women know that the stone had already been rolled away and that Jesus was alive.

But the women's question persists today. Who will roll away the stone for us? Who will free humanity from death, from sin, and from despair? How do we roll away the culture of death?

PRAYER. *Lord, renew my faith that the stone has been rolled back already and that Your victory is among us!*

 HEY stood still, their faces filled with sadness.

MAY 3

—Lk 24:17

REFLECTION. On the first Easter Sunday afternoon, the two disciples walking on the road to Emmaus failed to recognize Jesus when He started walking with them. Perhaps it was because they were so disheartened.

Often we are too absorbed in our own disappointment to see that hope is right in front of us. For many who are pregnant, despair and fear can lead to the violence of abortion.

PRAYER. *Lord, I pray for all whose sadness tempts them to abortion. Give me the courage to reveal Your loving presence to them.*

OW Thomas . . . was not with the rest when Jesus came.

—Jn 20:24

REFLECTION. So where was Thomas on that first Easter night? Perhaps he was out looking for Jesus! After all, he had to see things for himself.

Yet Thomas did not find Jesus until he returned to the community of Peter and the other Apostles. We too need the community of the Church united around the successor of Peter. There we find the strength to affirm life.

PRAYER. *Lord, keep me always in union with the Church and vigorous in proclaiming life!*

ELOVED, since God loved us so much, we should love one another.

—1 Jn 4:11

REFLECTION. When we obey the command in this verse of Scripture, we give life to one another.

When we love our unborn neighbors, we do all we can to save them from the violence of abortion. And in doing so, we are loving God Himself.

PRAYER. *Lord, inspired by Your generosity, help me to love those who may be difficult to accept or care for.*

"NEW feminism" affirms the true gift of women . . . while rejecting the imitation of forms of "male domination" . . . and seeking to eliminate every form of discrimination, violence, and exploitation. —*The Gospel of Life*, 99

REFLECTION. The early feminist leader Elizabeth Cady Stanton said, "When we consider that women are treated as property, it is degrading to women that we should treat our children as property to be disposed of as we see fit."

Authentic feminism is pro-life!

PRAYER. *Lord, renew our society with a deeper appreciation of the true genius of women and of their role in a culture of life.*

OR he had filled Jerusalem with innocent blood. — 2 Kgs 24:4

REFLECTION. The difficulties God's people encountered from the enemies around them were not the result of military or political flaws but of moral flaws. Chief among them was the shedding of blood by child sacrifice.

The strength of a people begins with its moral character and that of its leaders, as well as its fidelity to the Lord's Covenant.

PRAYER. *Lord, You hate the shedding of innocent blood. Protect and forgive Your people and bring us to the Promised Land of eternal life.*

T is I who bring both death and life.

—Deut 32:39

MAY 8

REFLECTION. Some people in our society use language about the *right to die* to disguise a *right to kill*—to get the burdensome and inconvenient out of our way.

No matter how frail they become, people are always children of God whose lives are valuable beyond measure.

PRAYER. *Lord, give us patience in our sufferings and a spirit of service when we encounter the sufferings of others.*

 ND from each man, too, I will demand an accounting for the life of his fellow man. —Gen 9:5

MAY 9

REFLECTION. We are accountable to God for many things. The first is life itself. God does not say here that we are simply accountable for our own life, as if we were each an island. He says we are responsible for the lives of others.

From the beginning, God makes us a community of persons not simply a collection of persons. And nobody is to be excluded.

PRAYER. *Father, turn our minds and hearts outward rather than inward toward a ceaseless care of others.*

CERTAIN idea of liberty which . . . has no regard for one's neighbor . . . ultimately becomes the freedom "of the strong" against the weak.

MAY 10

—*The Gospel of Life*, 19

REFLECTION. Cardinal Meisner of Germany compared the slaughter of tens of millions of unborn children by abortion to the genocide campaigns conducted by Hitler and Stalin.

Whenever a government removes equal protection from some human beings, it is an insult to all human beings. The class of victims may change, but the evil is the same.

PRAYER. *O Lord, preserve world governments from corruption and make them havens for human rights.*

HE breathed on them and said, "Receive the Holy Spirit."

MAY 11

—Jn 20:22

REFLECTION. On the first Easter night, Jesus breathes His Spirit upon the Apostles, that they too might bring new life out of the chaos and darkness of sin. A second Creation account is taking place here.

God "has sent the Holy Spirit among us for the forgiveness of sins" (Prayer of Absolution). The same Spirit Who causes sin to flee will cause death to flee, and His priests have a key role to play.

PRAYER. *Spirit of Life, we beg You to come. Bring order and beauty out of the chaos of sin.*

NOT even murderers are deprived of their dignity as persons.

—*The Gospel of Life,* 9

REFLECTION. If we ask, "How can we eliminate capital punishment?" The answer is, "Eliminate abortion."

As long as we throw away the innocent, it is quite hard to convince people not to throw away the guilty.

PRAYER. *Lord, may we protect the innocent, and may we not fail to recognize the dignity even of the guilty.*

THERE is one mediator between God and man, Christ Jesus, Himself a man.

—1 Tim 2:5

REFLECTION. Jesus is humanity's only mediator with God precisely because He is both Divine and human, and His humanity comes from Mary. All her importance flows from her Son, and our worship of the Son naturally leads to honoring His mother.

Marian devotion teaches us something about our pro-life commitment. *Mother and child belong together.* To hurt one is to hurt the other; to love one is to love the other.

PRAYER. *Mary, thank you for being the mother of Jesus Who now shares our humanity. Teach us to honor every mother and child.*

I N the beginning God created the heavens and the earth. Now the earth was formless and empty, darkness was over the surface of the deep, and the Spirit of God was hovering over the waters. —Gen 1:1-2

MAY 14

REFLECTION. The Spirit of God brought life and light out of chaos and darkness. The Holy Spirit is "the Lord and Giver of Life," and this is true both on a natural and supernatural level.

To worship the Holy Spirit, then, demands that we stand against all that destroys life.

PRAYER. *Holy Spirit, breathe on us and renew within us the fullness of life and the strength to defend it.*

T HE authorities are God's servants, and they devote themselves to this service. —Rom 13:6

MAY 15

REFLECTION. As Martin Luther King Jr. said, the law cannot get the white man to love me, but it can stop him from lynching me. Laws restrain evildoing.

They also have power to shape minds and hearts. When our children learn in school that something is legal, they are learning that such a thing is right. Whether regarding abortion or anything else, both hearts and laws must be changed.

PRAYER. *Father, give us a healthy respect for the power of law and a Spirit-filled determination to shape law according to Your will.*

74

THE blind man said to Him, "Rabbi, let me receive my sight."

—Mk 10:51

MAY 16

REFLECTION. People change when they *see* abortion. One wrote, "I was horrified by the gallery of photos of those tiny innocents—murdered, but I'm glad to have seen them. No one can truly form an opinion on abortion without seeing the horror. I had no idea the practice was so brutal."

PRAYER. *Lord, give Your people courage to face the evils around us so that we may have greater strength to fight them in Your Name.*

 PREACH the message; be persistent in doing so, whether in season or out of season; convince, reprove, and encourage, but with great patience and instruction.

—2 Tim 4:2

MAY 17

REFLECTION. Do you want to hear your parish priest talk more about abortion and the pro-life movement?

The first place to start is to listen to your priest and learn how he thinks. What is he most interested in and passionate about? Then, when you find out, link that issue with the abortion issue.

PRAYER. *Lord, bless our priests and all who preach and teach Your Word. Free their hearts and open their lips so that they may speak up for the defenseless.*

ID not He Who made me in the womb make them?

—Job 31:15

MAY 18

REFLECTION. In a Culture of Life we recognize that miscarriage is the loss of an actual child, who is a person.

Every reasonable effort should be made, therefore, to take the bodily remains of this child and commit them to the earth by a proper memorial service and burial. Such a witness is a significant step to building a culture of life.

PRAYER. *Father, I entrust to You today all children who died from miscarriage and ask You to console their families.*

F both you and the king who reigns over you follow the Lord your God—good!

—1 Sam 12:14

MAY 19

REFLECTION. Pro-abortion politicians will say to us, "My office does not deal with abortion." But their position on abortion tells us what they think of government: does it protect rights that come from God, or does it give those rights itself? Whether one will vote on abortion is beside the point.

Before we cast our vote for our leaders, we need to know what kind of authority they think we are giving them.

PRAYER. *Lord, keep our leaders aware of the difference between their role and Yours.*

ND they shall name Him Emmanuel, a name that means "God is with us."
—Mt 1:23

MAY 20

REFLECTION. In the midst of the abortion tragedy, the Church does not point fingers of condemnation. Rather, the Church extends hands of compassion and help to lift up out of despair those who are tempted to abort their children.

The Church informs her people of the many alternatives to abortion and says, "I am with you and will enable you to say 'yes' to life."

PRAYER. *Lord, may we reach out to those who are tempted to abort because they feel alone, that they may know that we and You are with them.*

HE requirements of the Law are inscribed in their hearts; and their own conscience will also bear witness for them.
—Rom 2:15

MAY 21

REFLECTION. Since the early '90s, over half of the freestanding abortion facilities in the United States have closed. Abortionists admit that one of the key reasons is that fewer doctors are willing to do abortions.

Despite all their money and influence, the abortion advocates have not succeeded in removing the stigma from abortion.

PRAYER. *Thank You, Father, for writing Your law on our hearts. May it strengthen us all in right conduct.*

HE human being is to be respected and treated as a person from the moment of conception. —*Donum Vitae*, 1

MAY 22

REFLECTION. Adult stem cell research has been going on for decades, and has proven helpful in treating various diseases. This research does not kill anyone.

Embryonic stem cell research only began in 1998 and does involve sacrificing a new human life in order to obtain the cells. The number of diseases that have been successfully treated with embryonic stem cells is zero.

PRAYER. *Lord, may the tiniest human beings be free from exploitation, and free us all from moral blindness.*

 ET everyone submit himself to the governing authorities, for there is no authority except that which derives from God. —Rom 13:1

MAY 23

REFLECTION. Abortion supporters say the government has no business telling us what we can do in the bedroom. But laws do prohibit theft, child abuse, or murder in bedrooms.

Moreover, abortions do not occur in the bedroom. They are committed in publicly advertised facilities. The government does in fact have the duty to stop such violence.

PRAYER. *Lord, I thank You for those who serve You in public office. Give our legislators wisdom to enact laws that preserve the rights of all.*

ER children arise and call her blessed; her husband also, and he praises her.
—Prov 31:28

MAY 24

REFLECTION. The early feminist leader Sara Norton said, "Perhaps there will come a time when the right of the unborn to be born will not be denied or interfered with."

Authentic feminism is pro-life because it takes seriously the message of equality—and that includes children.

PRAYER. *Lord, may all mothers see that their happiness lies in giving themselves away in love to their family and to You!*

E will not speak on his own authority, but he will speak what he hears . . . for he will take what is mine and communicate it to you.
—Jn 16:13-14

MAY 25

REFLECTION. The Holy Spirit is God, and all He says to us is consistent with what the Father and the Son have revealed. "The Holy Spirit . . . will . . . remind you of all that I told you" (Jn 14:26).

No disciple can claim the "freedom of the Spirit" to contradict the commandments, including that which forbids the killing of the innocent.

PRAYER. *Holy Spirit, fill the hearts of all people, that they may not believe any new or false gospels that justify the Culture of Death.*

IT IS necessary to nurture . . . a contemplative outlook...arising from faith in God, the author of life, who has "wonderfully made" each person . . . —*The Gospel of Life*, 83

MAY 26

REFLECTION. There are two ways to look at a tree: we can calculate the value of the lumber, or we can be moved by the beauty of the branches. Both views have their place, but our culture has gone overboard in calculating usefulness to the detriment of reverence.

This is especially dangerous when we look at human lives for their productivity rather than their dignity.

PRAYER. *Lord, fill us with wonder as we contemplate human life and all Your creation.*

WHEN a prayer or plea is made by any of your people . . . each one aware of his afflictions and pain . . . then hear from heaven . . .
—2 Chr 6:29-30

MAY 27

REFLECTION. Bertrand Russell once wrote, "A fisherman once told me that fish have neither sense nor sensation, but how he knew this, he could not tell me."

A practicing abortionist once told me that unborn children could feel no pain—but how he knew this, he could not tell me either. Research now suggests that babies in the womb feel pain much earlier than we thought.

PRAYER. *Lord, may the pain of these children awaken the consciences of Your people so that the killing may end.*

BEFORE the foundation of the world He chose us . . .

—Eph 1:4

MAY 28

REFLECTION. God's choice always comes before ours. We could not choose to be created because we were not there to do the choosing.

From all eternity, He took the initiative to make us and to save us. Our choices are secondary and are carried out in the context of His choice to give life and love.

PRAYER. *Father, thank You for the gift of our own free will. Protect it from corruption; may we always choose in You and for You.*

I HAVE set before you life and death, blessings and curses. Now choose life . . .

—Deut 30:19

MAY 29

REFLECTION. The early First Century document called the "Teaching of the Twelve Apostles" begins by saying, "There are two ways, one of life and the other of death, and great is the difference between the two."

It states, "Do not murder a child by abortion or kill a newborn infant." Throughout the centuries this teaching has been consistent.

PRAYER. *Lord, You have revealed the road of happiness to us and to our world. Keep us, in our laws and in our culture, on the path of life.*

TO hinder a birth is merely a speedier man-killing; nor does it matter whether you take away a life that is born, or destroy one that is coming to the birth. That is a man which is going to be one; you have the fruit already in the seed.

MAY
30

—Tertullian, *Apologeticum*

REFLECTION. The Lord's dominion over life—over the whole process of its coming and going—is the basis for our pro-life convictions.

To say "No" to life at any stage of its development is to say "No" to God Himself.

PRAYER. *Lord, may we rejoice in Your faithful care for life from its earliest stages.*

MARY set out and journeyed in haste into the hill country. . . . Mary remained with Elizabeth for about three months.

MAY
31

—Lk 1:39, 56

REFLECTION. After Mary was told she would be the mother of God, the truth of her new status did not distract her from Elizabeth's needs. Real encounters with God do not turn us into ourselves, but rather make us more responsive to the needs of others.

Religion does not keep us within the walls of our churches; rather, we go out to serve the needs of those whose lives and rights are in danger.

PRAYER. *Lord, may we learn from what Mary did. Send us to help mothers and children in need.*

JESUS Christ is the same yesterday, today, and forever.

—Heb 13:8

REFLECTION. The teaching of Christianity on the sanctity of life does not flow from some historical circumstance, political ideology, or changing opinion. It is based on the person of Jesus Christ Who does not change.

He is the perfect reflection of the Father, the source of all life. That is why the Church holds that its pro-life teaching "is unchanged and unchangeable" (*The Gospel of Life*, 62).

PRAYER. *Lord Jesus, give us the constancy and fidelity of perseverance to our pro-life commitment until the end of our journey.*

MAY He enable us to achieve what is pleasing to Him through Jesus Christ.

—Heb 13:21

REFLECTION. The pro-life movement is not primarily a response to *Roe v. Wade*. It is a response to Christ. This movement stands in the tradition of the early Christians who rescued abandoned infants from the streets, to those who worked to liberate slaves.

Jesus Christ came to free the oppressed; His disciples do the same.

PRAYER. *Jesus, I stand in a great tradition of disciples who have served the oppressed in Your name. Keep me strong in my response to You!*

E are unprofitable servants; we have only done our duty.

—Lk 17:10

JUNE
3

REFLECTION. The pro-life movement is not controlled "from above" or orchestrated through commanders giving orders.

The response to children in danger of being killed flows from our most basic human inclinations. This is why the movement is so large and diverse and why such diversity is legitimate.

PRAYER. *Lord, thank You for the pro-life movement that shows forth humanity at its best.*

HEN you come, bring along . . . the scrolls, particularly the parchments.

—2 Tim 4:13

JUNE
4

REFLECTION. One of the practical things we can do for the pro-life cause is to purchase some of the latest pro-life books and donate them to the public library.

You can be sure that abortion advocates fill the libraries with their books. Let's make sure our neighbors are receiving the pro-life message.

PRAYER. *God of all knowledge, give Your people a thirst for learning and a zeal to educate others in the message of life.*

AND for this I pray: that your love may increase ever more and more in knowledge and full insight. —Phil 1:9

JUNE
5

REFLECTION. After seeing photos of abortion, a teenager wrote, "I am a 15-year-old girl . . . I have looked at most of your website tonight and I must say that I am astonished. I knew that abortion was basically murdering your fetus, but I had no idea it was such a cruel process.

"Your pictures gave me the best image of what really goes on in abortion clinics."

PRAYER. *Lord, help Your people to love their unborn brothers and sisters by growing in knowledge of what threatens their lives.*

LET justice roll on like a river, righteousness like a never-failing stream!

—Am 5:24

JUNE
6

REFLECTION. Sometimes there is a tension between those who work to defend the right to life and those who work for "social justice." Yet there can be no social justice without establishing the most basic justice, the protection of one's life.

If the right to life is not secure, neither is any other right.

PRAYER. *Lord, enable Your people who work for what is right to resist every temptation to minimize or neglect any aspect of the demands of justice.*

S for the saints who are in the land . . . in them there is all My delight.

JUNE 7

—Ps 16:3

REFLECTION. God calls His people to work together for the cause of life and justice. Just as we cannot work in isolation from God, we likewise cannot work in isolation from one another.

Every laborer in the Lord's vineyard has something to learn from every other laborer, and together they lift one another up in times of weariness.

PRAYER. *Lord, keep us working hand in hand and in unity of heart for the purposes You inspire.*

 HESE commandments that I give you today . . . Tie them as symbols on your hands and bind them on your foreheads. Write them on the doorframes of your houses and on your gates.

JUNE 8

—Deut 6:6, 8-9

REFLECTION. Many states now have specialty license plates that have the words "Choose Life" above the plate number.

Money raised from the purchase of these plates supports alternatives to abortion, and the pro-life message is spread on the highway!

PRAYER. *Father, give us creativity to see more ways we can spread the message of life and courage and perseverance in using them!*

O home to your family and tell them how much the Lord has done for you, and how He has had mercy on you.

—Mk 5:19

JUNE 9

REFLECTION. Many pro-life activists have had abortions. They speak up for the children they once killed—and that is part of their healing.

Many of those in need of healing begin that journey because their conscience is stirred by those who expose the wounds of abortion.

PRAYER. *Lord, You inspire those who have found Your healing to carry out Your mission. Give fruitfulness to their words and works!*

T is written: "I believed and therefore I spoke," we also believe, and therefore speak.

—2 Cor 4:13-14

JUNE 10

REFLECTION. A Virginia High School senior was told he could not wear a sweatshirt that read, "Abortion is Homicide." However, after he sought legal help, the school allowed him to wear it.

The best way to defend our free speech rights is to exercise them without fear.

PRAYER. *Holy Spirit, open our lips to speak, even when that speech may upset others. Give us grace to defend our rights without fear.*

THE only honest stance . . . is that of radical solidarity with the woman.

JUNE
11

—John Paul II, *Crossing the Threshold of Hope*

REFLECTION. The difference between the pro-life and pro-abortion movements is not that we love the baby and they love the mother. The real difference is that they think you can separate the two and we say you can't.

You cannot kill a baby without hurting the mother, and you cannot protect the baby without loving the mother.

PRAYER. *Lord, You have called us to a love that recognizes the intimate union of mother and child. May they flourish together in love and protection.* _____

THEIR message goes forth throughout the earth, and their words to the ends of the world.

JUNE
12

—Ps 19:5

REFLECTION. The Internet provides one of the easiest and least expensive ways of spreading God's word.

Each of us can reach thousands of others by joining Internet discussion groups and blogs, and from the comfort of our own home, take a stand on the sanctity of life.

PRAYER. *Lord, we thank You for the technology that assists us to spread Your word to countless people.*

THOUGH the mind receives light and strength from faith, this issue belongs to every human conscience that looks for truth and is concerned about humanity. —*The Gospel of Life*, 101

JUNE 13

REFLECTION. Jesus, the Bible, and the Church teach that stealing is wrong. Does it follow that laws that prohibit stealing impose a religious belief on the rest of us? Of course not.

But some argue that a law protecting the unborn would impose religion. They think freedom of religion should allow child-killing.

PRAYER. *Lord, You have blessed human conscience with the ability to perceive that killing children is wrong. Increase the moral strength of Your people, that this evil may end.*

THEY maintain the appearance of godliness but deny its power . . . —2 Tim 3:5

JUNE 14

REFLECTION. Abortion supporters used to call it a decision between a woman and her doctor. Now they say it's a decision between a woman and her God.

They have run out of arguments to defend abortion, so they simply appeal to God as a way to shut down all argument.

PRAYER. *Lord, preserve us from the misfortune of turning to You without seeking You and of invoking You without listening to You.*

ND behold, I am with you always, to the end of the world.

—Mt 28:20

JUNE 15

REFLECTION. Abortion leads to isolation, despair, and a feeling of being abandoned by everyone. The Church, on the other hand, brings the assurance of Jesus: "I am with you."

The People of God, while rejecting abortion, embrace with love those who have had abortions and lead them to the healing mercy of Christ.

PRAYER. *Lord, reach into the darkness brought on by abortion, and enable Your people to bring the light of Jesus' presence to wounded hearts.*

———————

OU shall not misuse the name of the Lord your God, for the Lord will not hold anyone guiltless who misuses His name.

—Ex 20:7

JUNE 16

REFLECTION. This commandment does not simply mean we should not use God's name as a curse word. It also means that we should not invoke His name to justify evil practices.

Some abortion supporters do this, saying they support abortion *because of* their faith, or claiming that the Bible justifies killing the unborn.

PRAYER. *Lord, may we never abuse Your Name to justify what You abhor. Preserve the purity of our worship and the integrity of our prayer.*

FOR You created all things; by Your will they were created.

—Rev 4:11

JUNE 17

REFLECTION. Cloning advocates make a misleading distinction between "reproductive" cloning—that is, actually bringing clones to birth—and "therapeutic cloning"—that is, using the clone's cells, but killing the clone before he or she is born.

In reality, *all* cloning is reproductive because the unborn clone is human, and *no* cloning is therapeutic because no medical benefit has been demonstrated.

PRAYER. *Father, You alone can create human life. Preserve us from the temptation of trying to do what You alone can do.*

IF only my anguish could be weighed . . . It would surely outweigh the sand of the seas.

—Job 6:2-3

JUNE 18

REFLECTION. Those who have had abortions are more likely to be tempted to suicide. The mother may see death as the only way of being reunited with her child and escaping the daily pain that the abortion brings.

"I deprived my child of life," she thinks, "and therefore I don't deserve my own."

PRAYER. *Lord, send Your Spirit upon all who are tempted to suicide and refresh them with new hope.*

91

AZE upon the birds . . . Are you not of far greater value than they?

—Mt 6:26

JUNE 19

REFLECTION. In Florida you can see signs on the beach that say, "Do not touch the sea turtles or their eggs. They are protected by local, state, and federal law."

If we do not have the right to choose to smash the egg of a sea turtle, why do we have the right to choose to smash a baby?

PRAYER. *Lord, we worship You as the source of everything that is. Teach us to value creation and to value humanity even more.*

HEY cannot sleep till they do evil; they are robbed of slumber till they make someone fall.

—Prov 4:16

JUNE 20

REFLECTION. Hundreds of taped phone conversations show abortion clinics throughout the nation deliberately failing to report the sexual abuse of minors. This is a flagrant violation of ethics and law.

When we lose sight of the sanctity of life, our concern for other aspects of the moral law is likewise weakened. One can't practice vice virtuously.

PRAYER. *Lord, protect all those who may become victims of the malice and negligence of the abortion industry—not only the unborn babies but their vulnerable young mothers.*

OUR light must shine so that it can be seen by others.

—Mt 5:16

JUNE 21

REFLECTION. A preacher once wrote that there is no such thing as secret discipleship. Either the discipleship will destroy the secrecy, or the secrecy will destroy the discipleship.

That's why being pro-life cannot just be a personal, private conviction. If it's in our heart, it needs to be on our lips and in our actions.

PRAYER. *Lord God, may I never try to be a secret disciple, but rather be proud to be known as one of Yours.*

N their lawlessness, bloodshed follows bloodshed.

—Hos 4:2

JUNE 22

REFLECTION. If a mother has the right to choose to kill her innocent, unwanted child, why doesn't the adult child have the right to kill her innocent, unwanted mother?

The "right to die" movement has nothing to do with people wanting to die. It has everything to do with people wanting to kill those whom they believe would be better off dead.

PRAYER. *Lord, I affirm today the primacy of life over choice. May every choice be guided and guarded by the immeasurable value of life.*

WHEN the child grew older, she took him to Pharaoh's daughter and he became her son. She named him Moses. —Ex 2:10

JUNE 23

REFLECTION. Many couples are eager to adopt children but are unable to do so, either because of burdensome laws, or because the children have been killed by abortion.

The pro-life movement promotes adoption; the pro-abortion movement does everything it can to discourage it.

PRAYER. *Lord, look with love on all those who seek to adopt a child. Bless them for their generous desire to give a child a loving home.*

GOD intended it for good to accomplish . . . the saving of many lives. —Gen 50:20

JUNE 24

REFLECTION. One of the simplest ways to stop abortions is to go to the facilities where the abortions happen and talk to the women who are walking in.

"Sidewalk counseling" is legal in every state, and has saved countless lives. Training is available from pro-life organizations.

PRAYER. *Lord, may You give all sidewalk counselors grace and wisdom, patience and perseverance. Save many lives and souls through their loving intervention.*

ND when He comes, He will prove the world wrong about sin and righteousness and judgment. —Jn 16:8

JUNE 25

REFLECTION. Here is the reaction of a "pro-choice" person upon seeing what abortion is: "I have looked at the pictures on this site on aborted babies and I started to cry. I have always believed in freedom of choice but after seeing this, I have to say this is just murder."

PRAYER. *Lord, Your Holy Spirit teaches us about You, and helps us to see the full truth about what is right and wrong. May that Spirit reveal to our world its sin and its salvation.*

HAT strength do I have, that I should still hope? What prospects, that I should be patient? —Job 6:11

JUNE 26

REFLECTION. Studies have shown that those who aborted their first pregnancy were four times more likely to engage in subsequent drug or alcohol abuse than those who never had an abortion.

Sometimes this behavior is aimed at dulling the pain abortion brings, or it is done because the mother feels unworthy of being protected, safe, and healthy.

PRAYER. *Lord, heal the spirits of those who feel unworthy of life and give them new hope.*

HEY lead my people astray, saying, "Peace," when there is no peace, and because, when a flimsy wall is built, they cover it with whitewash. —Ezek 13:10

REFLECTION. Talk about giving mixed signals. Late-term abortionist George Tiller tells couples who come to him to abort, "The hard part is saying goodbye to the hopes, dreams, and relationships that you have with your baby."

He even has a chaplain who conducts spiritual services and baptisms for the children who are killed.

PRAYER. *Lord, have mercy. Move to repentance those who misuse the faith of others to justify wrongdoing, and heal all those who turn to You.*

NE of the soldiers thrust a lance into His side, and immediately a flow of blood and water came forth. —Jn 19:34

REFLECTION. We worship Jesus' heart. It is the core of the pro-life movement, which is a movement of self-sacrificing love.

Nothing can stop the love of the Heart of Jesus, which is the meaning of the flame we see. This love is met by rejection and hatred, symbolized by the wound in the heart.

PRAYER. *Lord, when my love for the unborn is met with misunderstanding, ridicule, and persecution , fill my heart with Yours, that I may continue to love those who cannot love me back.*

ND I will ask the Father, and He will give you another Advocate to be with you forever, the Spirit of Truth.

JUNE
29

—Jn 14:16-17

REFLECTION. Our Lord referred to the Holy Spirit as *another* advocate, the first one being Jesus (1 Jn 2:1). Because we cannot save ourselves, we need an advocate to plead for our forgiveness and salvation.

What, then, does the Holy Spirit do when He comes to them? He makes us advocates for the helpless!

PRAYER. *Come, O Spirit Advocate. Give speech to my tongue to always defend vulnerable human lives!* _____

VEN if my father and mother abandon me, the Lord will gather me up.

JUNE
30

—Ps 27:10

REFLECTION. Blessed Margaret of Castello (13th c.) is Patron of the Unwanted. When her parents, who were respected nobility, discovered at her birth that she was a badly deformed dwarf, hunchback, and blind, they refused to give her a name, locked her up in a small cell, and eventually abandoned her while traveling.

Had we known what Margaret's parents were doing to her, would we have spoken up?

PRAYER. *Blessed Margaret, pray that we may speak up for the unwanted.*

97

AY the Lord cause your love to increase and overflow for one another and for everyone else.

JULY 1

—1 Thes 3:12

REFLECTION. The Pope and bishops have told us that we are not to "accommodate ourselves" to laws permitting abortion.

This means much more than simply not having or participating in an abortion. It means not letting anything keep us from loving and defending the unborn.

PRAYER. *Lord, let my love overflow all boundaries, that I may resist anyone's effort to limit my love for those who are in danger of death.*

 F anyone does sin, we have an Advocate with the Father, Jesus Christ, the Righteous One.

JULY 2

—1 Jn 2:1

REFLECTION. Often, we tend to think that God is advocating *against* those who have committed sins against human life and dignity.

Scripture tells us, however, that if we sin, He advocates *for us*—not, of course, to justify the sin, but *to justify us*, to bring us reconciliation, healing, and salvation. This is true precisely because of the dignity of the human person.

PRAYER. *Lord, as we steadfastly oppose sins against human life and dignity, may we steadfastly proclaim Your mercy and healing.*

THE Lord watches over the stranger and sustains the fatherless and the widow.

—Ps 146:9

JULY 3

REFLECTION. The Statue of Liberty is a strong symbol of the welcome our nation has given to people from around the world. On its base are the words of Emma Lazarus, "Give me your tired, your poor, your huddled masses yearning to breathe free."

This welcome can make no sense if we are afraid to welcome the children in the womb.

PRAYER. *Lord, fill our hearts with a spirit of welcome for born and unborn alike.*

JESUS spoke to men a message of peace, and taught us to live as brothers. His message took form in the vision of our fathers as they fashioned a nation where men might live as one. This message lives on in our midst as a task for men today and a promise for tomorrow. —Preface, Liturgy for Independence Day

JULY 4

REFLECTION. The pro-life work we do advances the purpose of today's celebration.

As a nation under God, we gather to give thanks and to pray for liberty and justice for all.

PRAYER. *Lord, grant the blessings of liberty to our unborn brothers and sisters.*

99

O now, Father, glorify Me in Your presence with the glory I had with You before the world began.

JULY 5

—Jn 17:5

REFLECTION. What was different about Jesus' glory after He ascended to heaven than when He was in heaven before coming to earth? Now, He is in heaven in a human body and soul—the same human nature that you and I share.

The Ascension teaches the world the meaning and destiny of human life: We are called to be in the heights of heaven.

PRAYER. *Lord Jesus, You took our humanity to the heights of heaven. When that same humanity is abused and rejected, may we lovingly respond.*

———————

 ith firm trust you should entrust your child to the Father and to His mercy. —John Paul II to those who have had abortions, *The Gospel of Life*, 99

JULY 6

REFLECTION. Baptism is the ordinary way to be born into God's grace. But for those killed without baptism, we can still have sure hope. St. Paul wrote that God wants all to be saved.

Let us entrust these children to the Lord, Who does not forget anyone that He creates, even when we do.

PRAYER. *Father, to You we commend the souls of all children killed by abortion. Bring them to heaven and bring us Your comfort.*

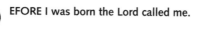

EFORE I was born the Lord called me.

—Isa 49:1

REFLECTION. When someone is pregnant, she is *not* "expecting a child"—she already has one. She is *not* "going to be a mother"—she already is a mother. The baby is *not* "on the way"—the baby has already arrived.

If we are going to change the way society treats unborn children, we have to change the way we talk about them.

PRAYER. *Lord, thank You for my brothers and sisters now alive in their mothers' wombs. May we all speak and act in a way that recognizes they are already among us!*

IVE to Caesar what is due to Caesar and to God what is due to God.

—Mt 22:21

REFLECTION. When asked whether taxes should be paid to Caesar, Jesus said the coin belongs to Caesar, for it bears Caesar's image. What then belongs to God? Human beings, because they bear God's image!

The implication of the passage is that what belongs to God includes Caesar himself! Caesar must obey God.

PRAYER. *Lord, bless all those in civil authority, that they may obey Your Divine and eternal law holding all life as sacred.*

THE people of Judah have done evil in My eyes, declares the Lord . . . They have built the high places . . . to burn their sons and daughters in the fire.

JULY 9

—Jer 7:30-31

REFLECTION. A woman who saw the photos of aborted babies on the Priests for Life website wrote to us, "Let me state first that I am rarely if ever speechless, I am very outspoken and speak what I feel. The abortion images are jolting, and will haunt me the rest of my life. . . . I will never be silent about this matter again."

PRAYER. *Jolt us, Lord; awaken us, and preserve us from sin.*

HE consoles us in all our afflictions and thereby enables us to console others in their tribulations.

JULY 10

—2 Cor 1:4

REFLECTION. Terri Schiavo's family now assists other families who face tragedies similar to their own and is calling for laws in various states to protect the disabled from being dehydrated to the point of death as Terri was.

Rather than being absorbed in bitterness or despair, this family has accepted from the Lord their mission to be a voice for the voiceless. *A Life that Matters* is their personal account of what happened to Terri.

PRAYER. *As I battle the culture of death, Lord, may I receive and share Your consolation.*

SHALL accept whatever they will do to me provided they save the child.

—St. Gianna Molla

REFLECTION. In 1962, Saint Gianna Beretta Molla died after giving birth to her fourth child. A physician herself, she understood the risks of her pregnancy, but refused abortion.

Some question her decision, given that she already had three children. However, nothing would have harmed those children more than if she had aborted their sister, and nothing blessed them more than the example of a mother who gave her life for her child.

PRAYER. *Saint Gianna, pray for us, that we may imitate your selfless love.*

 HEREFORE, just as you received Christ Jesus the Lord, continue to walk in Him.

—Col 2:6

REFLECTION. Imagine a person who accepts the Host at Communion, and then breaks off a piece, hands it back, and says, "Except this piece, Father!" This is what the person who rejects other people may as well do.

In receiving Christ, we are to receive the *whole* Christ, in all our brothers and sisters, whether convenient or inconvenient.

PRAYER. *Lord, may all Your people who have received You in Communion receive one another with unconditional welcome.*

LORD, do not withhold Your mercy from me . . . my sins have so engulfed me that I cannot see . . . and my heart sinks within me. —Ps 40:12-13

JULY 13

REFLECTION. A woman who had an abortion wrote, "I was deceived by all I had read or heard. . . . It was a rough procedure. I knew as soon as my uterus was violated that I had participated in a murder. My spirit fragmented and the evil that was in that clinic came in all around me. I lost my mind."

PRAYER. *I lift up to You, Lord, all those enduring mental anguish from their abortion. Send Your Spirit to heal them.*

 FTER sending them all outside, He . . . entered the room where the child was . . . and said to her . . . "Little girl, I say to you, arise!" —Mk 5:40-41

JULY 14

REFLECTION. When a fire is reported, the firemen do not sit around the fire house and have a prayer service. They go to where the fire is. When a priest gets a sick call, he goes to the bedside of the sick person.

The same is true with abortion. We are called to show up at the places where the killing occurs. This expresses solidarity with them in their hour of greatest need.

PRAYER. *Enable Your people, O Lord, to give each other the gift of presence.*

THERE is a time for everything . . . a time to be born and a time to die.

—Eccl 3:1-2

JULY 15

REFLECTION. Advocates of euthanasia use terms like "help in dying." But this blurs the distinction between *giving assistance to a dying person* and *causing their death*.

Mother Teresa "helped" many people "in dying." She was present to them, helping them find courage to face death, reminding them of their dignity, preparing them to meet the Lord. This is the legitimate meaning of *helping people to die.*

PRAYER. *Lord, may we show the dying their dignity and Your compassion.*

BE fruitful and increase in number; fill the earth and subdue it.

—Gen 1:28

JULY 16

REFLECTION. The single largest destroyer of human life in our nation and in the world is not poverty or AIDS; it is not heart disease or cancer; it is not terrorism or war. It is abortion.

Some 50 million children around the world are killed each year by this procedure.

PRAYER. *O Lord, enable us to pursue those things that will preserve our species and continue to fulfill Your original command to multiply.*

AS for Mary, she treasured all these words and pondered them in her heart.

—Lk 2:19

REFLECTION. The Rosary has conquered countless enemies, and many pray it in front of abortion mills.

As we acknowledge Jesus as the fruit of Mary's womb, we stand to pray for our brothers and sisters in the womb. As we honor the greatest mother, we pray for all the frightened mothers.

PRAYER. *Mary, our Mother, bring us Jesus yet again; lead us to His victory over all forms of death.*

THEY do more harm to those who practice them than to those who suffer from the injury.

—*Gaudium et Spes,* 27

REFLECTION. This quote from Vatican II is speaking about abortion, euthanasia, genocide, and various other forms of violence against human life and dignity.

It obviously calls for a deep concern for the welfare of those who carry out these activities. The Church seeks both the protection of the victims and the salvation of the perpetrators.

PRAYER. *Lord, have mercy on those who carry out practices against human life and dignity. Convert, heal, and save them.*

FOR here we have no lasting city, but we are seeking the One that is to come.

—Heb 13:14

REFLECTION. The Church has always held that the State does not contain the fullness of human hope or embrace the totality of human existence. The State rather, exists for the human person, not the other way around.

That is why governments either have to protect human rights, or have to be reformed. Human law is always subject to Divine law.

PRAYER. *Lord, as I strive for my heavenly home, I thank You for my earthly home; may I work to improve it.* _____

ROE v. Wade must be reversed.

—US Bishops, "A Matter of the Heart"

REFLECTION. Some say that because of Roe v. Wade, abortion is a settled issue. But it is no such thing. Roe v. Wade did not "settle" abortion any more than the Dred Scott decision "settled" slavery, or the "Plessy v. Ferguson" decision "settled" segregation.

Those evils were defeated precisely because we are a nation that thirsts for equality and justice, and that thirst cannot be quenched or extinguished by a Supreme Court decision.

PRAYER. *Thank You, Lord, for the vigor You inspire in Your people to resist injustice.*

AVE no fear. The outcome of the battle for life is already decided.

—John Paul II, World Youth Day, Denver, 1993

REFLECTION. Despite how powerful the culture of death seems, we foster in ourselves and others, an uninterrupted confidence that the tools of grace with which God has equipped the People of Life are far more powerful.

We do, at the same time, have to be faithful to our own role in proclaiming, celebrating, and serving that victory.

PRAYER. *Thank You, Lord, for conquering death and for giving us what we need to counteract its destructive power in our day.*

 IGHT from fertilization is begun the adventure of a human life.

—*Donum Vitae*, n. 1

REFLECTION. Never has there been a more unscientific debate than the one about embryonic stem cell research. There is no disease that embryonic stem cells have been able to treat.

Science is based on evidence. If there is no evidence that embryonic stem cells can help, why do people continue to call for the killing of embryos in order to harvest those cells?

PRAYER. *Lord, may all researchers and scientists grow as strong in their moral character as their technical knowledge.*

HERE must be a deep unity among the works of charity on behalf of life . . . for at each of its stages and conditions, human life is sacred and inviolable, a gift that is indivisible.

JULY 23

—*The Gospel of Life, 87*

REFLECTION. The consistency of our care for life flows from the fact that God's care is constant.

Every life at every stage of its existence belongs to Him. God's rights over human life are never interrupted or diminished.

PRAYER. *God of uninterrupted love, keep us constant and consistent in our care for one another.*

 HE Lord sustains the poor, but humbles the wicked in the dust.

JULY 24

—Ps 147:6

REFLECTION. In 1941 German Cardinal Clemens von Galen preached against the Nazi euthanasia program.

He declared, "These numerous cases of unexpected death in the case of the insane are not natural, but often deliberately caused, and result from the belief that it is lawful to take away life which is unworthy of being lived . . . Once admit the right to kill unproductive persons . . . then none of us can be sure of his life."

PRAYER. *Inspire Your preachers, Lord, with the courage we see in Cardinal von Galen.*

THAT which came to be found life in Him.

—Jn 1:3

JULY 25

REFLECTION. On this day in 1968, Pope Paul VI issued *Humanae Vitae,* which means, "Of Human Life." That encyclical outlines the Church's vision of human life, marriage, and the connection between human love and the creative action of God.

Love leads to life; it does not close it off. Love welcomes life; it is not afraid of it. Love and life go together because they are two aspects of the one God.

PRAYER. Lord God, You are love and You are life. Open all people to Your love so that they may give life.

I HAVE . . . seen the misery of My people in Egypt. I have heard them crying out because of their slave drivers, and I am concerned about their suffering.

—Ex 3:7

JULY 26

REFLECTION. Some abortion supporters say to us, "Let's agree to disagree."

We have the greatest respect for those who disagree with us. But when victims are oppressed, we don't just "agree to disagree" with the oppressor. Rather, we intervene to *stop the oppressor* and save the victim.

PRAYER. Lord, You hear the cry of the oppressed; may we hear it also and respond.

HAVE come to call not the righteous but sinners.

—Mk 2:17

JULY 27

REFLECTION. Some abortion supporters seek "common ground" with pro-lifers. Jesus Christ ate and talked with sinners, and yet also warned them strongly to repent of their sins.

There is no room for compromise about abortion, but there must always be room to talk to people about it.

PRAYER. *Lord, teach us the wisdom of dialogue that does not compromise, and of respect that does not equate evil with good.*

HUMAN being, in distinction to animals and things, can in no way be dominated by anyone.

—*The Gospel of Life*, 19

JULY 28

REFLECTION. If representatives of the Church abuse children, the State steps in. The Church likewise has a duty to intervene when the State allows abortion.

America is proud of its freedom of religion, and of its protection of human rights. The two can go together, as long as "separation of Church and State" never means that either one looks the other way when human rights are violated.

PRAYER. *Lord, may both Church and State be faithful in their duty to protect human rights.*

111

PRIEST happened to be traveling along that same road, but when he saw him he passed by on the other side.

—Lk 10:31

REFLECTION. Perhaps the priest and Levite walked by the victim on the roadside because they thought the robbers were around the corner waiting to attack them. They asked, "If I stop to help this man, what will happen to me?"

The Samaritan reversed the question and asked, "If I do not stop to help this man, what will happen to him?"

PRAYER. *Lord, may I stop calculating the risk to myself, and instead ask what will happen to the vulnerable if I don't help them.*

 ONE of us lives for himself, and none of us dies for himself. If we live, we live for the Lord, and if we die, we die for the Lord. Therefore, whether we live or die, we are the Lord's.

—Rom 14:7-8

REFLECTION. There are two basic truths that each person has to admit in this life: 1. There is a God. 2. It isn't me. To understand these lessons is to understand why evils like contraception, abortion, and euthanasia are wrong.

Only God has absolute dominion over human life and over its coming and going.

PRAYER. *In life and death, O Lord, abide with me. I am Yours.*

THE Spirit Himself bears witness with our spirit that we are children of God.

—Rom.8:16

JULY 31

REFLECTION. The Holy Spirit, the Spirit of Truth, enables us to understand created realities, their value, and their relationship to the Creator and to our own happiness.

We can therefore ask the Holy Spirit to give us an understanding of the value and dignity of the human person.

PRAYER. *Through Your eternal Spirit, You enable me to understand Your works as coming from Your hand. I praise You forever!*

JESUS holds a perpetual priesthood . . . He has the full power to save those who approach God through Him, since He lives forever to intercede for them.

–Heb 7:24-25

AUG. 1

REFLECTION. In the heights of heaven, where He sits at the right hand of the Father, what does Jesus do?

Scripture tells us that, sharing our human nature, He constantly intercedes for us. He presents to the Father the dignity of our humanity, that it may be filled with the life of God.

PRAYER. *Lord, give us confidence that we can always approach You as You intercede in Your humanity for ours.*

THEN will the words that are written be fulfilled: "Death has been swallowed up in victory." —1 Cor 15:54

REFLECTION. At the scene of the first murder of Abel by Cain, the soil "opened its mouth" to swallow Abel's blood (Gen 4:10-11). At the scene of the final victory of life, it is death itself that will be "swallowed up in victory."

God is in the business of destroying death, and that is why His people work on behalf of life.

PRAYER. *Lord, continue to give us consolation amidst a Culture of Death, that this evil will not last forever but will be swallowed up in victory.*

EVERYONE shares responsibility for . . . developing . . . legislative initiatives that . . . will help build . . . a society that recognizes the dignity of every human being.
—*The Gospel of Life*, 90

REFLECTION. The law called the "Born Alive Infants Protection Act" states that babies born alive at any time of gestation, even as a result of a failed abortion, are to be treated as persons under the law.

Protecting unwanted babies after a failed abortion brings us one step closer to protecting them before an abortion.

PRAYER. *Lord, please hasten the progress being made in our laws for the protection of life!*

ROE v. Wade effectively rendered the definition of human personhood flexible and negotiable.

AUG.
4

——"Living the Gospel of Life," 10

REFLECTION. In the Supreme Court case Sierra Club v. Morton, Justice Douglas wrote, "The ordinary corporation is a 'person.' . . . So it should be as respects valleys, alpine meadows, rivers, lakes, estuaries, beaches, ridges, groves of trees, swampland, or even air."

A few months later, he agreed with the Roe v. Wade decision saying that unborn children are *not* persons.

PRAYER. *Lord, free us from the mindset that can assert personhood for almost everything except human beings.*

I PUT to death and I bring to life.

AUG.
5

—Deut 32:39

REFLECTION. No religion and no pro-life group advocates that we are obliged to take every single treatment and procedure available to keep us alive. Foregoing a worthless treatment is not, and should not be called, euthanasia or suicide.

Yet while there are such things as worthless treatments, there is no such thing as a worthless life. We may reject a treatment; we must never reject a life.

PRAYER. *Give your peace, O Lord, to all who are dying today.*

UDDENLY, there were two men talking with Him, Moses and Elijah.

—Lk 9:30

AUG. 6

REFLECTION. Jesus was transfigured; the glory of His divinity shone through His humanity, which reminds us that humanity always expresses the image of God.

The Transfiguration was meant to remind the Apostles that death would not have the last word.

PRAYER. *Jesus, may Your Transfiguration be a powerful reminder that You have brought about a new kingdom of life.*

OU will know the truth, and the truth will set you free.

—Jn 8:32

AUG. 7

REFLECTION. A woman wrote to us, "I have a dear friend who is very pro-choice and I said: 'Have you ever seen what an abortion looks like?' The answer was: 'No.' I showed her the pictures on the Priests for Life website.

"She was rightfully and truly horrified about what this REALLY looks like. And, she started to cry. She isn't pro-choice anymore."

PRAYER. *You are truth, Lord Jesus, and in You we find the truth about everything. Assist us to expose the truth about abortion.*

PART from Me you can do nothing.

—Jn 15:5

AUG. 8

REFLECTION. Prayer is union with God. Prayer and action are not two separate options but rather two aspects of union with God.

When we come away from prayer we should not feel rested but restless. We should not feel that we've done our duty but that we've been given our duty.

PRAYER. *Lord, You are a consuming fire, the source of all activity. Keep me rooted in prayer and strong in action.*

HEN He saw the crowds, He had compassion on them because they were distressed and helpless like sheep without a shepherd.

—Mt 9:36

AUG. 9

REFLECTION. At times, we have all "aborted" God's will in our lives. We never look down on those who have committed the sin of abortion or who promote it. They are not the enemy but rather are *captive to the enemy.*

We seek to free them, as their brothers and sisters who are no strangers to temptation, error, and sin.

PRAYER. *God of compassion, fill me with the same compassion You have for me and for all who have sinned.*

117

HOEVER gives even a cup of cold water to one of these little ones . . . will not go unrewarded.

AUG. 10

—Mt 10:42

REFLECTION. As Terri Schiavo was dying, a police officer was in the room at all times, making sure that nobody gave Terri a drop of water. A vase of flowers sat on her night table. Those flowers were being nourished and a human being was not.

How upside-down is the Culture of Death! How offensive is the cruelty we show to the weak and vulnerable.

PRAYER. *Have mercy on Your people, Lord; bring an end to the cycle of blindness and violence around us.*

 HEREFORE strengthen your feeble arms and weak knees. Make level paths for your feet.

AUG. 11

—Heb 12:12-13

REFLECTION. A woman wrote to Priests for Life, "Up until I visited this site I had been pro-choice. . . . After seeing the images on your site, there was no decision to be made. I figured that whatever hardships having a baby at this time would bring me would be far easier than living with the guilt if I was to get an abortion. The pictures had such a powerful effect on me. They helped me to be strong."

PRAYER. *Thank You, Lord, for the strength that comes from knowing the truth.*

UCH is the complete confidence in God **AUG.** that we have through Christ. . . . Our **12** competence comes from God Who has empowered us . . . —2 Cor 3:4-6

REFLECTION. The same Holy Spirit who created the universe, descended upon the womb of Mary, came as tongues of fire at Pentecost, and leads the Church on her mission is the One Who calls and equips us for our pro-life work.

Let us not lack for a moment the confidence and joy that come from Him and impel us to build a Culture of Life.

PRAYER. *Come, Holy Spirit, and equip us, just as You equipped disciples of every century to advance the Gospel of Life.*

 OD did not give us a spirit of timidity **AUG.** but rather a spirit of power and of love **13** and of wisdom. —2 Tim 1:7

REFLECTION. Our pro-life work requires constant courage, which is nurtured through Scripture, incessant prayer, and the example of saints and other historical figures who fought against the injustices of their times.

When we feel we don't have courage, we should simply do what we would do if we did.

PRAYER. *Lord, at times I ask what I should do next, but I already know. I simply need the courage to do it. Grant it to me today.*

 LL generations will call me blessed.

—Lk 1:48

REFLECTION. Mary's Assumption, which we celebrate tomorrow, is a sign that God ultimately saves us—and will raise us—in body and in soul.

Some who justify abortion say they don't know if the child has a soul. But what matters is that the child has a body, and when we know that abortion destroys the body, we have all the information we need to know it's wrong.

PRAYER. *Mary, I rejoice in your Assumption, and in the hope to which it points, that we will all enjoy eternal freedom from death.*

 HE Mighty One has done great things for me.

—Lk 1:49

REFLECTION. In the human family, which God decided to join, there can be no closer bond than mother and child. They belong together; their destinies are intertwined.

That is one of the central messages of the pro-life movement. To love and care for a mother necessarily means protecting, loving, and caring for her child.

PRAYER. *Blessed Virgin Mother, on this day of joy we honor you. Pray for us and for the victory of life!*

120

HY direct action? Why sit-ins, marches and so forth? Isn't negotiation a better path? . . . Indeed, this is the very purpose of direct action. . . . to dramatize the issue that it can no longer be ignored.

AUG. 16

—Dr. Martin Luther King, Jr., "Letter from Birmingham Jail," April 1963

REFLECTION. There are strong parallels between the Civil Rights Movement and the Pro-life Movement. One of them is that the powers with whom we must negotiate do not see the need. Peaceful protest is therefore required.

PRAYER. *Lord, may Your people faithfully protest injustice and awaken those in power.*

OU will be doing well if you truly observe the sovereign law . . . "You shall love your neighbor as yourself."

AUG. 17

—Jas 2:8

REFLECTION. Some politicians claim that it is not their business to impose their religious beliefs on the rest of America, but none object to enforcing laws against stealing. Why isn't that an imposition on religion, given the fact that the Bible tells us not to steal?

The reason, of course, is that you have a right to your possessions, not because you are a Christian, but because you are human.

PRAYER. *Lord, help us distinguish between religious beliefs and moral laws rooted in our nature.*

LL things were created through Him and for Him.

AUG.
18

—Col 1:16

REFLECTION. Cloning is an assault on human dignity and a denial of God's purpose for human life.

It's about starting new lives in order to harvest cells for the purported benefit of the person who is genetically identical. In the process, of course, the embryo would be killed.

PRAYER. *Lord Jesus, may we rejoice in the truth that we were created through You and for You and oppose whatever contradicts it.*

OR see what earnestness this godly sorrow has produced for you . . . what indignation . . . what desire to see justice done.

AUG.
19

—2 Cor 7:11

REFLECTION. Christians believe in righteous anger, which the Lord and His Saints exhibited in the face of evil. We are angry at what the culture of death does each day.

We ask the Holy Spirit not to *extinguish* our anger but rather to *channel it* into a wholesome, energized passion which sustains us in the task at hand.

PRAYER. *Give me righteous anger, Lord, purified by Your Spirit.*

WITHOUT a doubt, contraception and abortion are, morally speaking, specifically different evils . . . the latter negates the virtue of justice and directly transgresses God's command, "You shall not kill."

— *The Gospel of Life,* 13

REFLECTION. Abortion and contraception are both grave sins, but the Pope points out that they are different in nature and that abortion is worse.

Neither should be tolerated.

PRAYER. *Free us, Lord, from the contraceptive mentality that closes the door to generosity.*

SHOUT it aloud, do not hold back. Raise your voice like a trumpet!

— Isa 58:1

REFLECTION. In order to give voice to the voiceless and to reach the numbers of people we need to reach in the short time we have to reverse the culture of death, we sometimes have to be in the public spotlight.

"Let your light shine before others," the Lord said, always reminding us that the glory goes to the Father (Mt 5:16).

PRAYER. *Lord, teach me that humility does not mean I am always hidden, but rather, that I am always exactly where You need me to be.*

HE said to His mother, "Woman, behold your son." Then He said to the disciple, "Behold, your mother." —Jn 19:26-27 **AUG. 22**

REFLECTION. Today we observe the Queenship of Mary, acknowledging that the highest place that any creature holds in heaven is occupied by a woman and a mother.

To be pro-life is to be pro-woman, and Mary the Mother of God is an inspiration for all women about how to embrace the vocation of motherhood, facing the unexpected with faith, courage, and joy.

PRAYER. *Queen of heaven, grant all your people a deep appreciation of the dignity of women, of motherhood, and of life.*

HE will have pity on the lowly and the poor; the lives of the needy He will save. —Ps 72:13 **AUG. 23**

REFLECTION. Biblically speaking, the "poor" are not simply those who are materially deprived, but rather those who have no help but God. God has mercy especially on those who realize He is their only hope and only help.

Those who are like God also have a "preferential option for the poor." In other words, we go first to those who need our help the most.

PRAYER. *Lord, I pray for the "poor," for those most abandoned and forgotten. Let their voices be heard and their lives spared.*

GOD . . . set me apart even before my birth.

—Gal 1:15

AUG.
24

REFLECTION. Many pro-abortion public officials say they believe that life begins at conception, but that they say they cannot legislate that belief on those who think it begins later.

But suppose someone said, "I believe that life begins at birth, but I cannot legislate my beliefs on those who think it begins later." Then the newborn would lose their legal protection.

PRAYER. *Lord, give our legislators and all Your people wisdom to know the difference between legislating beliefs and protecting lives.*

BEHOLD, children are a gift from the Lord, a reward of the fruit of the womb.

—Ps 127:3

AUG.
25

REFLECTION. Because children are a "gift," they can neither be demanded nor discarded. That is why it is wrong not only to abort them, but also to "create" them through artificial means that replace normal human procreation.

We do not have a "right" to children, but rather an awesome privilege to receive them, if God so chooses to give the gift.

PRAYER. *Lord, deepen our understanding of children as a gift. Give generosity to all parents and patience to all those who await that gift.*

125

HOEVER Loves Me will keep My word, and My Father will love him, and We will come to him and make Our abode with him. —Jn 14:23

AUG. 26

REFLECTION. When the Father and Son come and abide with us, it is through the Holy Spirit. The Spirit unites the human family in bonds of self-giving love.

Abortion and other manifestations of the culture of death, however, divide the human family because they are the opposite of self-giving.

PRAYER. *Holy Spirit, we need You and we long for the unity You bring. Give us the love that overcomes division.*

 HAVE gazed upon You in the sanctuary so that I may behold Your power and Your glory. —Ps 63:3

AUG. 27

REFLECTION. The baby in the manger and the man on the cross do not look like God; yet by faith we know Jesus is no mere man. The Eucharist does not look like Jesus, but we worship Him.

Christians are used to looking beyond appearances. Hence we can also see in the annoying person, or the person who is unconscious in a hospital bed, or in the unborn child, the image of God.

PRAYER. *Holy Spirit, grant us to see beyond appearances to the dignity of every life!*

OU have made us for Yourself, O Lord, and our hearts are restless until they rest in You. —St Augustine

AUG. 28

REFLECTION. These famous words of St. Augustine remind us what the Church means by saying human life is "sacred."

As human persons, we are uniquely capable of having a relationship with God. Our lives are oriented to Him as our final goal and fulfillment; hence we cannot be owned by others, manipulated, or discarded.

PRAYER. *Lord, I rejoice in my ability to relate to You, and I honor every human being as Your own special possession.*

HE king . . . had John beheaded in the prison. —Mt 14:9-10

AUG. 29

REFLECTION. St. John the Baptizer, who leaped for joy in Elizabeth's womb, preached a message of repentance to those in power. He told King Herod that it was wrong for him to have his brother's wife and was killed as a result.

John is an example for us to speak the truth boldly. Being a Prophet is not primarily about telling the future but about pointing out what God says about what is happening now.

PRAYER. *St. John the Baptizer, pray that we may boldly proclaim the right to life for all people.*

127

EUTHANASIA is a serious violation of Divine Law.

—*The Gospel of Life, 65*

AUG.
30

REFLECTION. If the terminally ill have a *right* to escape *their* suffering, why shouldn't teenagers have a right to escape theirs? After all, isn't this equal protection under the law? Moreover, why should people be able to exercise a right only when they can articulate it?

Voluntary euthanasia *automatically* introduces *non-voluntary* euthanasia.

PRAYER. *Enable us, Lord, to bear our suffering in union with You.*

BE mindful, O Lord, that mercy and kindness have been Yours from of old. Remember not the sins of my youth.

—*Ps 25:6-7*

AUG.
31

REFLECTION. A woman wrote of her abortion, "It was very painful, physically and mentally. It affected me in the worst way. I felt very guilty. I couldn't look at any kids. I know I won't ever do it again."

Those getting an abortion think it will solve their problems, and they find out it only creates more of them.

PRAYER. *Lord, show us how to reach out to those who have had abortions and how to understand their pain. Bring us all to healing.*

UCH attacks strike human life when it is most frail and defenseless. What adds to their gravity is that these attacks are normally carried out within the core of, and with the participation of, the family, which by its very nature is designed as the "sanctuary of life." **SEPT.**

1

—*The Gospel of Life*, 11

REFLECTION. Not all sins against life are the same. Context matters. Greater dependence calls for greater protection. The family setting implies greater compassion.

PRAYER. *God of the family, Lord of the frail, may compassion and protection overflow from Your heart to ours!*

 MID all the crimes one can commit against life, procured abortion has characteristics that render it especially grave and detestable . . . yet in our day . . . people have gradually lost sight of how serious it is. **SEPT.**

2

—*The Gospel of Life*, 58

REFLECTION. A woman who saw the photos of aborted babies wrote, "OH MY GOSH. I just read your entire web page. OH MY GOSH is all I can really say out loud. I have seen articles and read about abortions before—but I still felt like it was the woman's decision. My mind was changed TODAY."

PRAYER. *Lord, grant light and conversion to all about abortion.*

129

TEACHING them to observe all that I have commanded you . . .

—Mt 28:20

SEPT.
3

REFLECTION. Pro-abortion politicians will often say to us, "Abortion is the law of the land." But the "law of the land" can be changed, just as it was changed regarding slavery and segregation.

The law of the land is meant to protect the good of the people. Because imperfect people make the law of the land, they sometimes make mistakes and allow things which experience later proves are not good for the people.

PRAYER. *Holy Spirit, come and renew the face of the earth; make us agents of change.*

THE human person is the measure of the dignity of work.

—*Compendium of the Social Doctrine of the Church,* 271

SEPT.
4

REFLECTION. The Church teaches that work has its final goal in the human person. In other words, people are not to be considered as just cogs in a wheel of productivity.

Work exists for people; it is an expression of the person and builds up his or her dignity. This is a key conviction in a Culture of Life.

PRAYER. *Lord, thank You for the contributions workers have made to the strength, prosperity, and well-being of our country.*

F we allow a mother to kill her own child, how can we tell people not to kill each other? —Mother Teresa of Calcutta

SEPT. 5

REFLECTION. Mother Teresa died on this day in 1997. She saw in each person—no matter how sick or depraved—the image of God. She spoke boldly to those in power about the evil of abortion. In her Nobel Peace Prize lecture, she said that the greatest destroyer of peace is abortion.

She led women away from abortion clinics and toward alternatives. Let us honor her by imitating her.

PRAYER. *Mother Teresa, pray for us so that we may defend life as you did.*

 OU will show me the path to life; You will fill me with joy in Your presence. —Ps 16:11

SEPT. 6

REFLECTION. Many men and women who have lost children to abortion are speaking publicly about their experience through the Silent No More Awareness Campaign (a project of Priests for Life and Anglicans for Life).

This campaign shows the harm abortion does, leads people to healing, and reveals the power and mercy of Christ.

PRAYER. *Lord, bless all the men and women who are speaking out about their abortion experiences. Thank You for their courage.*

ALL of them look to You to give them their food at the appropriate time.

—Ps 104:27

SEPT.
7

REFLECTION. Reflection: One of the myths that was used to kill Terri Schiavo was the idea that food and water are medical treatments. But when we come back from a meal, we don't say, "I just had my latest medical treatment." Rather, we say, "I had breakfast, lunch, or dinner."

Food and water are ordinary means of care which may not be taken away from the sick.

PRAYER. *Lord, I pray today for all who need assistance to receive nourishment. Protect them and surround them with people who care.*

SHE was found to be with child through the Holy Spirit.

—Mt 1:18

SEPT.
8

REFLECTION. Today we celebrate the Birthday of the Blessed Virgin Mary, chosen by God to be His own mother.

We need Mary's example more than ever because so many mothers are afraid to be mothers, and so many opinion-makers in our society have forgotten what motherhood really means.

PRAYER. *Mary, I pray for all who are pregnant and afraid that they may find new hope and strength to say "Yes" to God's plan as you did.*

HE and her whole household had been baptized.

—Acts 16:15

SEPT. 9

REFLECTION. Baptism shows that we are always called to give a welcoming "Yes" to life, and never the harsh "no" of abortion.

The so-called "pro-choice" message is that we choose whom we will care for. Baptism teaches us that we are responsible for those whom God has chosen first.

PRAYER. *Lord, I welcome each and every person You have chosen to create. May they share Your life abundantly.*

 F the Spirit of Him Who raised Jesus from the dead dwells in you, then the One Who raised Christ from the dead will also give life to your mortal bodies through His Spirit that dwells in you.

—Rom 8:11

SEPT. 10

REFLECTION. The Holy Spirit gives life, bringing forth creation at the beginning of time, descending upon Mary to bring about the Incarnation, bringing forth the Eucharist from mere bread and wine, and descending upon the graves of God's people to raise them from the dead.

PRAYER. *Holy Spirit, come and work through Your people to build the Culture of Life. Keep us close to You; fill us with Yourself.*

ELIVER us from the evil one.

—Mt 6:13

SEPT.
11

REFLECTION. The evil of September 11, 2001 was not simply that lives were lost, but that some human beings had a blatant contempt for the right of other human beings to live. The same contempt for human life is found in every abortion clinic.

What moral difference does it make if the instrument of death is an airplane or surgical forceps? The evil we fight is a reflection of the evil we do.

PRAYER. *Lord, on this sad anniversary I resolve to defend all life, whatever threatens it.*

OU will be my treasured possession.

—Ex 19:5

SEPT.
12

REFLECTION. Dr. James McMahon was an abortionist in Southern California and performed partial-birth abortions.

When asked by the American Medical Association news how he justified doing it, he admitted that the baby was a child, but there was a more important matter, "Who owns the child?" "It's got to be the mother," he explained.

PRAYER. *Lord, nobody but You is the owner of human life. Keep us mindful that we are servants and that You alone are our Master.*

THUS democracy . . . becomes totalitarianism. No longer is the State the home where all are considered equal; rather it is a tyrant State, which thinks it can kill its weakest and most defenseless members. —*The Gospel of Life*, 20

SEPT. 13

REFLECTION. Some see laws permitting abortion as a minor flaw; the Pope is saying here that they change the very nature of the state.

PRAYER. *Lord, free us from the tyranny of governments that think they can dispose of human life.*

E also glory in our sufferings. —Rom 5:3

SEPT. 14

REFLECTION. Today is the Feast of the Triumph of the Holy Cross. Because His death destroyed our own, the Cross is a symbol of ultimate triumph over evil and a symbol of the cross we must embrace in everyday life.

Especially if we work to save the unborn, we are subject to ridicule and rejection. Our plans for pro-life activity should not be geared towards avoiding rejection but rather should count on it.

PRAYER. *Lord, may we see the cross as our triumph, today and forever.*

135

ND you yourself a sword will pierce.
—Lk 2:35

SEPT.
15

REFLECTION. Today we honor Mary under the title of Our Lady of Sorrows. Mary's heart was pierced with a sword many times, most notably at the foot of the Cross.

The Sorrowful Mother is also a symbol of the many mothers who feel they cannot continue their pregnancies, as well as those who have aborted a child. Mary intercedes for them today, and so must we all.

PRAYER. *Our Lady of Sorrows, pray for us and for all mothers who bear pains of body and soul.*

HE winds blew and buffeted that house. And it collapsed with a great crash.
—Mt 7:27

SEPT.
16

REFLECTION. Pro-abortion politicians will say to us, "Abortion is just one of many issues; I embrace a consistent ethic of life."

The foundation of a house is only one of many parts of the house, but it is essential to build the other parts. That is why the bishops teach that the right to life is the foundation of all human rights, and that our priority must be fighting abortion.

PRAYER. *Lord, You warned against building our house on sand. May the right to life itself shape all our efforts for justice.*

N this rock I will build My Church, and the gates of the netherworld will not prevail against it. —Mt 16:18 **SEPT. 17**

REFLECTION. In a battle, gates do not run out onto the battlefield to attack the enemy. Rather, they protect the city from the enemy.

When Jesus says these gates will not prevail against the Church, it is the Church doing the attacking; the Church is storming the gates, advancing the Kingdom of Life!

PRAYER. *Lord, give us confidence that the gates of falsehood will fall in the presence of truth.*

 PECIFICALLY in the "flesh" of each human being, Christ continues to show Himself to us and to lead us into communion with Him, so that to repudiate a human life in any way is truly to repudiate Christ Himself.—*The Gospel of Life,* 104 **SEPT. 18**

REFLECTION. For some people religion is too "religious." They think they encounter or reject Christ only when speaking or thinking about Him explicitly, or only when doing or failing to do specifically religious activities.

But the Church teaches clearly that we meet or reject Jesus in each human life.

PRAYER. *Jesus, You are all around us. Open our eyes to Your presence in every human life.*

137

THE greatest destroyer of peace is abortion.

—Mother Teresa (Nobel Peace Prize Lecture)

SEPT.
19

REFLECTION. You have heard people say that being wrong on abortion outweighs being right on other issues, and that is correct. The full truth is, if you are wrong on abortion, *you can't be right* on other issues.

To permit abortion, but then to cry out for the right to work, housing, education, health care, and peace is to say that these other rights belong to some people but not to all.

PRAYER. *Lord, forgive our nation for allowing all the rights of the unborn to be taken away.*

YOU cannot partake of the table of the Lord and the table of demons.

—1 Cor 10:21

SEPT.
20

REFLECTION. Some public officials who refuse to oppose child-killing continue to receive Holy Communion. But communion means union.

To desire union with Jesus is to desire union with life, and to be in communion with His teachings means to *accept* them. When we come to Jesus, we are the ones who have to change to be like Him.

PRAYER. *Lord, give us the strength to be in union with You and therefore to reject evil practices.*

YOU restored me to health and let me live. **SEPT. 21**

—Isa 38:16

REFLECTION. Pro-abortion politicians will say, "I support women's rights and health." That is why they should examine the evidence that abortion is destructive of women's health.

That is also why they should examine how the abortion industry, through unregulated and dangerous clinics, continues to deceive and exploit women.

PRAYER. *Lord, bring healing to those who have been injured, physically and emotionally by abortion, and awaken our public officials to the harm abortion does.*

THROUGH Him all things came into existence. **SEPT. 22**

—Jn 1:3

REFLECTION. *Humanae Vitae* is much more than a "birth control" encyclical. It declares and reaffirms the very meaning of human life as a sacred gift from God.

We find our fulfillment precisely in welcoming, nurturing, and giving ourselves away for that gift of life. By capturing this vision of life, prohibitions on abortion and contraception make sense as pieces of a greater picture.

PRAYER. *Jesus, You fill the world with life. Take away our fear and make us fruitful.*

139

O not use your freedom as a means to cover up wrongdoing.

—1 Pet 2:16

SEPT. 23

REFLECTION. The public debate should not be whether the bishops will allow politicians to receive communion, but whether the politicians will allow children to be aborted.

When we read the descriptions of what the abortion procedure does to little babies, we understand that the core question is not whether these politicians are good Catholics, but whether they are decent human beings.

PRAYER. *Lord, I pray today for every leader, politician, and person who remains blind to the evil of abortion.*

CTUALLY, this is just a pitiful imitation of legality; it contradicts, at its very foundation, the ideal of democracy, which can only be real when it acknowledges and protects the dignity of every human life.

—*The Gospel of Life*, 20

SEPT. 24

REFLECTION. Simply because a law may be passed "in the proper way" does not automatically mean it is legitimate.

Authentic law serves the good of people, and the protection of their rights.

PRAYER. *Lord, may legislators and judges see the foundations of authentic law.*

I MUST confess that I am not afraid of the word "tension." I have earnestly opposed violent tension, but there is a type of constructive, nonviolent tension which is necessary for growth. —Dr. Martin Luther King, Jr., "Letter from Birmingham Jail," April 1963

SEPT. 25

REFLECTION. Pro-life people likewise must not be afraid of "tension."

When there is the false peace of a society that has accommodated child-killing and the killing of the disabled and terminally ill, then the solution requires constructive tension.

PRAYER. *Lord, You brought about the tension of the Cross and the tension of salvation. May Your followers reject false peace and work for true justice.*

———————

TAKE warning, O rulers of the earth. Serve the Lord with fear . . . —Ps 2:10-11

SEPT. 26

REFLECTION. Pro-abortion politicians say, "The government should not be involved in a personal decision like abortion." But the government got "too involved" in abortion when it claimed to have the authority to authorize it.

Some say it is none of the government's business to prohibit abortion. Actually, it is none of the government's business to permit abortion.

PRAYER. *Instill in our civic leaders, O God, the proper fear of Your kingship. May they realize the limits of their authority.*

PPOSITION to abortion and euthanasia does not excuse indifference to those who suffer from poverty, violence and injustice. . . . But being "right" in such matters can never excuse a wrong choice regarding direct attacks on innocent human life.

—"Living the Gospel of Life," 23

SEPT. 27

REFLECTION. Consistency cuts both ways, and challenges those with blind spots to human rights.

The most common mistake is to tolerate child-killing while advocating for adults.

PRAYER. *Lord, free us from ever trying to use justice as an excuse for injustice, or right as a justification for wrong.*

AR broke out in heaven, with Michael and his Angels in combat against the dragon.   —Rev 12:7

SEPT. 28

REFLECTION. The devil and his followers thought they could be like God by their own choice. But Michael's name means "Who is like God?" Only God's choice can exalt us to His throne.

The battle between pro-life and pro-choice is the same battle. Some think their own choice, rather than God's, determines right and wrong.

PRAYER. *Sovereign Lord, may all acknowledge that You alone are God, and that Your choice, not our own, exalts us.*

THE Angel said to her, do not be afraid, Mary.

—Lk 1:30

REFLECTION. Such is Gabriel's message today to every pregnant mother. "Do not be afraid" to welcome new life, even when it upsets your plans, changes the direction of your life, and requires you to mature in unexpected ways.

If God creates a life in the womb, He is making you ready, and has plans for that child and for you.

PRAYER. *Lord, remove all fear from the hearts of those who are pregnant, and fill them with Your peace and joy.*

THE Gospel of God's love for humanity and the Gospel of the dignity of each person and of his life, are one and the same indivisible Gospel.

—*The Gospel of Life,* 2

REFLECTION. Some who preach the Gospel think that pro-life activity is a "hobby," added onto the Gospel. It is not. It is as integral to the Gospel as any cause or activity could be.

The Gospel is all about the redemption and exaltation of the human person, and the marriage of humanity and divinity in and through Christ.

PRAYER. *Lord Jesus, may we never lose our awe at the destiny Your Gospel announces for humanity.*

HOLD the keys to death.

—Rev 1:18

OCT.
1

REFLECTION. The alternative to accepting death is to try to control it by giving ourselves the authority to take life. Hence we have abortion, infanticide, and euthanasia. Just take control. Eliminate suffering by eliminating the person.

"Euthanasia" is killing. As such, it contradicts the fact that God is God.

PRAYER. *Lord, You are in control of my life, my suffering, and my death. May I never forget that.*

T must be his Angel.

—Acts 12:15

OCT.
2

REFLECTION. God assigns an Angel to watch over us at every moment of our lives. Each unborn child has a Guardian Angel, too.

If God cares enough about each unborn child to create that child and then assign him or her an Angel, then certainly He expects us also to exercise some care and vigilance to speak up for and protect the lives of those children.

PRAYER. *Send Your Angels, O Lord, to assist all who are tempted to abort, and to all who work to persuade them to choose life.*

YOU are the light of the world. A city built upon a mountain cannot be hidden.

—Mt 5:14

OCT.

3

REFLECTION. In elections, each of us has but one vote. Yet we can all influence *thousands* of votes. And we should start with the people who need the least amount of urging—those who already agree with us on the key issues of the day, and who would probably support the candidates we support.

Let's reach for the "low-hanging fruit," thereby getting more results for the energy we expend.

PRAYER. *Lord, let me not miss the opportunities You give me to mobilize Your people to do good!*

MY brothers, birds, you should praise your Creator very much and always love Him. . . . —St. Francis of Assisi

OCT.

4

REFLECTION. St. Francis preached to the birds about God's care: "He gave you feathers to clothe you, wings so that you can fly, . . . though you neither sow nor reap, He nevertheless protects and governs you without any solicitude on your part."

If such a message is true for birds, it's true for the tiniest human beings, those yet unborn. God loves them, and so must we.

PRAYER. *St. Francis, pray for us, that we may have reverence for all creation.*

145

AS far as the east is from the west, so far has He removed our transgressions from us.
—Ps 103:12

REFLECTION. Today is the Feast of St. Faustina, to whom Jesus revealed the wonders of divine mercy. The Chaplet of Divine Mercy was given to her especially because of the sin of abortion.

God revealed to her that because of this evil, the world needs His mercy more than ever. He even permitted St. Faustina to suffer special pains, representing the pain of abortion.

PRAYER. *For the sake of His sorrowful passion, have mercy on us and on the whole world!*

SEEK justice, encourage the oppressed. Defend the cause of the fatherless.
—Isa 1:17

REFLECTION. Some say, "I'm personally opposed to abortion, but can't impose my views on others." But laws don't regulate "views," they regulate behavior. Someone's "view" may be that you should not be protected. But the law provides you that protection anyway.

The unborn should enjoy the same protective benefit of the law, despite anyone's "views."

PRAYER. *Lord, help our nation to protect the unborn, despite the fact that some do not acknowledge their value.*

"**B**LESSED is she who believed that what the Lord has said to her would be fulfilled."

—Lk 1:45

REFLECTION. The Rosary is a devotion strongly embraced by the pro-life movement. In the Hail Mary we praise a mother, and we worship the fruit of her womb. Our salvation began because a mother said yes to the life within her!

In the Rosary we also say, "Pray for us sinners." We know that sin is in the world, but we start by repenting of the sin within us. That is the best way to rebuild the Culture of Life.

PRAYER. *Holy Mary, Mother of God, pray for us sinners, now and at the hour of our death.*

AMONG important issues involving the dignity of human life . . . abortion necessarily plays a central role . . . . Its victims are the most vulnerable and defenseless. . . .

—US Bishops' Pastoral Plan
for Pro-life Activities, 2001

REFLECTION. The bishops continued: "This focus and the Church's commitment to a consistent ethic of life complement one another."

Consistency does not mean all issues are of equal weight; it means all people are of equal value.

PRAYER. *Lord, give us the wisdom to meet the greatest needs with the greatest sense of urgency.*

PHYSICIANS and health care workers are also responsible, when the skills they acquired to promote life are placed at the service of death. —*The Gospel of Life, 59*

REFLECTION. Pro-abortion politicians will often say to us, "Legislators should not be practicing medicine." But we're not asking them to practice medicine, but to prevent the *abuse* of medicine.

Medicine is for the purpose of preserving life; abortion takes life. There is no disease that abortion cures, and no proven medical benefit.

PRAYER. *Lord, may all doctors practice medicine to preserve life.*

YOU are at my side, with Your rod and Your staff that comfort me.
—Ps 23:4

REFLECTION. Some want "living wills" in order to make their wishes known regarding medical treatment.

The better solution is a health care proxy, that is, a person you appoint to speak for you if you cannot speak for yourself. Such a person can consult doctors and clergy when the actual circumstances arise, rather than making treatment decisions today for circumstances nobody can foresee.

PRAYER. *Lord, You are already in our future; be our protection and comfort each day.*

O one can have greater love than to lay down his life for his friends.

—Jn 15:13

REFLECTION. Jesus Christ made the sacrifice of Himself "through the eternal spirit" (Heb 9:14).

It is in the Holy Spirit that we too have the power to love, which consists in giving ourselves away for the good of the other. Such is to be our response to the unborn and to all the vulnerable.

PRAYER. *Lord, may the world see us, Your disciples, giving our very lives to other human beings. Seeing this love, may they discover and receive the Spirit Who inspires it.*

 HE Lord said to me, "Do not say, 'I am only a child.' You must go to everyone I send you to and say whatever I command you."

—Jer 1:7

REFLECTION. Many of the youth involved in the pro-life movement are motivated by the fact that they could have been aborted. As they speak up for the unborn, they are really speaking up for themselves.

We reaffirm that they are persons not because they are wanted, but because of the dignity they receive from their Creator.

PRAYER. *Lord, bless the survivors of abortion and make them mighty witnesses for life.*

LOOKED, and there was a pale green horse. Its rider was named Death.

—Rev 6:8

OCT. 13

REFLECTION. Our Lady of Fatima warned that without conversion, Russia would spread its errors throughout the world, leading to the annihilation of nations. That was in 1917.

Three years later, Russia first legalized abortion—and that error has indeed spread worldwide and continues to annihilate some 50 million children a year.

PRAYER. *Lord, You have warned us of evils, and You have also promised salvation. Protect us; save us; raise us up.*

 HOEVER observes the whole Law but trips up on a single point is held guilty of breaking all of it.

—Jas 2:10

OCT. 14

REFLECTION. Suppose a political candidate said that although he personally opposed terrorism, he thought the terrorists had a right to do what they did. What kind of support do you think this candidate would have?

Certain positions of candidates are so clearly contrary to the good of the nation that the candidate's other positions, although good, do not matter.

PRAYER. *Spirit of Wisdom, fill Your people, their candidates, and their leaders.*

THE failure to protect and defend life in its most vulnerable stages renders suspect any claims to the "rightness" of positions in other matters . . .

—"Living the Gospel of Life," 23

REFLECTION. Why do the bishops say that when public servants disregard the right to life, their stand for other human rights is "suspect?" The reason is that the right to be safe, free, educated, and economically secure, cannot be human rights if life itself isn't a human right.

To make one's humanity negotiable means that other rights that flow from one's humanity are negotiable, too.

PRAYER. *Lord, make the humanity and rights of all Your people secure.*

BUT when her baby is born, she no longer recalls the suffering, because of her joy that she has brought a child into the world.

—Jn 16:21

REFLECTION. St. Gerard Majella (18th c.) is the Patron Saint of pregnant mothers, of childbirth, and of unborn children.

Thousands of children have been named after St. Gerard by parents who are convinced that it was his intercession that helped them to have healthy children.

PRAYER. *St. Gerard, intercede for mothers who are having difficulties in pregnancy and childbirth, and show us how to help them.*

151

A LL authority in heaven and on earth has been given to Me.

—Mt 28:18

REFLECTION. What if a Church said that as part of its worship service it would sacrifice a little child on the altar? Certainly the State would step in to stop that, and few people would regard that as an infringement of the separation of Church and State.

Neither is it an infringement when the Church tells the State it cannot authorize the killing of children by abortion.

PRAYER. *O God, You are Lord of both Church and State. Grant that neither infringe upon the human rights of Your people.*

S PEAK up for those who cannot speak for themselves, for the rights of all who are destitute. —Prov 31:8

REFLECTION. The ministry of Jesus shows a preferential option for the poor and weak, and the Church therefore inherits this as her own priority. The work of peace, justice, and life gives preference to those whom society has marginalized, and those who cannot defend themselves.

These ministries are, essentially, a voice for the voiceless—whether those voiceless are oppressed nations, the poor, the terminally ill, or the unborn.

PRAYER. *Thank You for the voice You give me, Lord. May I use it for those who have none.*

HATEVER you did for one of the least of these brethren of Mine, you did for Me. —Mt 25:40

OCT. 19

REFLECTION. Christ is the One in prison and on the sickbed, who either gets a visit from us or is ignored; Christ is the One Who is hungry and thirsty, Who is the immigrant and the One on death row.

And Christ is the child Who is in the womb, in danger of the abortionist's knife.

PRAYER. *Lord, let us truly see You and feel Your presence in each and every human person. May that presence spur us on to generous service.*

N what way can one still assert that all people have dignity while the killing of weaker and more innocent people is allowed? —*The Gospel of Life,* 20

OCT. 20

REFLECTION. Pope John continued: "In the name of what justice is the most unjust of discriminations practiced: some individuals are held to be deserving of defense and others are denied that dignity? When this happens, the process leading to the breakdown of a genuinely human co-existence and the disintegration of the State itself has already begun."

Abortion is not just an "issue." It deteriorates the very foundations of civilization.

PRAYER. *Preserve our society, Lord, by freeing it from legal abortion.*

"**D**ELIVER us, Lord, from every evil, and grant us peace in our day. . . . "

—Order of Mass

REFLECTION. Peace is a fragile gift, and a key characteristic of the culture of life. We pray for peace in the midst of every Eucharist, and we work to remove the obstacles to receiving peace.

Reverence for life opens the way to peace; truth and justice provide its foundation; relationships of mutual love preserve it.

PRAYER. *Grant us peace, Lord, as well as the courage to defend life. May government leaders and their citizens rejoice in Your peace.*

THE common outcry, which is justly made on behalf of human rights—for example, the right to health, to home, to work, to family, to culture—is false and illusory if *the right to life,* the most basic and fundamental right and the condition of all other personal rights, is not defended with maximum determination.

—*Christifideles Laici,* 1988

REFLECTION. It is an illusion to support human rights and also support abortion.

When the State fails to protect the right to life, it has destroyed its reason to protect any rights.

PRAYER. *Make us consistent, Lord, in advocating for all the rights of Your people.*

HERE, O death, is your victory? Where, O death, is your sting?
—1 Cor 15:55

OCT. 23

REFLECTION. A woman who saw the photos of aborted babies on the Priests for Life website wrote to us, "I had once strongly believed in pro-choice, but after reviewing this website, I am all for Pro-Life. I just recently found out that I am five weeks pregnant . . . . I cannot imagine me doing this to my baby."

PRAYER. *You continue to dispel the myths, O Lord, that allow violence to continue. Make us courageous vehicles of Your truth.*

"COME now, let us reason together," says the Lord. "Though your sins are like scarlet, they shall be as white as snow; though they are red as crimson, they shall be like wool."
—Isa 1:18

OCT. 24

REFLECTION. A woman wrote, "After the abortion, I felt dirty, ashamed, like a low ant below all else. I felt betrayed, like a betrayer. Something which took such little time left a permanent scar.

"I sat in the rain the rest of the day, occasionally walking, crying, and not knowing why I really had the abortion."

PRAYER. *Come, God of hope; lift up all burdened by their abortion. Make them whole again.*

155

VERY man has the obligation to vote, because by voting he can determine . . . who will make tomorrow's laws either to be unjust and perverse, or to promote human values. . . God Himself asks that every Christian, make his contribution by voting.
OCT. 25
—Bishop Karl Romer,
Pontifical Council for the Family

REFLECTION. Everything we can say about the tremendous moral responsibility of those who craft legislation and put it into effect really reflects the moral responsibility of those who put them in those positions in the first place—the voters.

PRAYER. *Lord, may we use wisely the freedom to elect our lawmakers.*

 AITHFUL Christians have a duty to participate in society . . . by voting so that they may advance the common good. And this duty must be taken seriously by Christians.
OCT. 26
—Bishop Elio Sgreccia,
Pontifical Academy for Life

REFLECTION. The Lord does not save us in isolation, but in community, and commands us to seek the good of the community in which we live.

Participation in the civil process simply reflects the solidarity God calls us to have with others, rooted in the call to justice, love, and service.

PRAYER. *Father, You bring Your people together. Help me respond by full participation in civic life.*

ET us never grow weary in doing what is right.

—Gal 6:9

OCT. 27

REFLECTION. Sometimes the moral obligation to vote is stronger than at other times. This is especially true when pro-life people can elect, in a close race, someone who will protect the unborn, and remove from office someone who won't.

Among candidates who have a strong enough base to win, we have a moral obligation to vote in such a way that will do the most to advance the culture of life.

PRAYER. *Lord, let me not miss the opportunity to advance what is good and right.*

E get the public officials we deserve. Their virtue—or lack thereof—is a judgment not only on them, but on us.

—"Living the Gospel of Life," 34

OCT. 28

REFLECTION. This powerful statement points to our responsibility to elect pro-life candidates and keep pro-abortion candidates out of office. They cannot get into office, of course, without a sufficient number of people voting for them.

Voters need to ask, "If a politician can't respect the life of a little baby, how is he supposed to respect mine?"

PRAYER. *Lord, raise up in our nation wise and virtuous voters, that we may have godly leaders.*

E urge our fellow citizens to see beyond party politics, to analyze campaign rhetoric critically, and to choose their political leaders according to principle, not party affiliation or mere self-interest.

OCT. 29

—"Living the Gospel of Life," 34

REFLECTION. Politics, though messy, is an opportunity to shape society according to moral principles. Voters must prayerfully discern which leaders will serve them well.

The inability to discern that attacks on life like abortion and euthanasia are evil should disqualify a candidate.

PRAYER. *Lord, shine through the eclipse of conscience that afflicts many public officials and give them wisdom.*

E encourage all citizens . . . to embrace their citizenship not merely as a duty and privilege, but as an opportunity meaningfully to participate *in building the culture of life.*

OCT. 30

—"Living the Gospel of Life," 34

REFLECTION. Voting is a moral obligation. In a representative form of government, the obligations Scripture places on kings and rulers belong to the voters.

The obligation to advance the culture of life by one's vote springs from one's obligation to the good of the nation and to the well-being of all the other citizens who live in it.

PRAYER. *Lord, give us a deep commitment to participate in the political process.*

EVERY voice matters in the public forum. Every vote counts. Every act of responsible citizenship is an exercise of significant individual power. We must exercise that power in ways that defend human life, especially . . . the unborn, disabled or otherwise vulnerable.

OCT. 31

—"Living the Gospel of Life," 34

REFLECTION. The Presidential race of 2000 was decided by fewer votes than are present in most parishes on a Sunday morning. Many other races are decided by literally a handful of votes.

Citizens easily underestimate the power of their vote.

PRAYER. *Lord, may I never fail to exercise my right to vote!* _____

LOVE the Lord, all His Saints.

—Ps 31:24

NOV. 1

REFLECTION. Many of the Saints we honor today were martyrs. But what is the difference between martyrdom and suicide? It is the difference between giving and taking.

In suicide, one takes his own life, pretending to be the master of it. In martyrdom, one realizes that only God is master of his life, and that he cannot hold on to that life at the cost of betraying God.

PRAYER. *Lord, as we honor Your Saints, grant that we may build a world that acknowledges You alone as the Master of life and death.*

159

ISRAEL, put your hope in the Lord, both now and forevermore.

—Ps 131:3

REFLECTION. The month of November is dedicated in a particular way to praying for the dead. This includes children who died before birth.

These children did not have the opportunity to be baptized; the Church teaches, however, that we can entrust them with confidence to the mercy of God.

PRAYER. *Lord, You love aborted children even more than we do. We entrust them to Your mercy.*

HE Holy Father speaks of the protection of life as the fundamental realization and respect for human rights. Without that realization, without that respect for the right to life, no other discussion of human rights can continue.

—Cardinal Renato Martino,
Pontifical Council for Justice and Peace

REFLECTION. Talk is cheap, and often it's worse than that. The very thing which we support in speech, we sometimes destroy by our actions.

So it is with those who fail to protect the unborn. That failure contradicts everything else they say about human rights.

PRAYER. *Father, fill all nations with respect for life, the foundation of all rights.*

E are . . . sorrowful, yet we are
always rejoicing.

—2 Cor 6:8, 10

REFLECTION. Life is joyful, and defending life is
a mission that should be carried out with joy.

We seek to foster, in ourselves and others, a
"joyful sorrow," that is, a spirit that is always
mourning because of its keen awareness of the
ongoing, unseen destruction of human life, and
at the same time, is always serene and rejoicing
that death has been conquered by Jesus Christ.

PRAYER. *Father, give us sorrow over the evils in
the world and joy as we fight them in union with
You.*

HERE are six things the Lord hates,
seven that are detestable to Him:
haughty eyes, a lying tongue, hands that
shed innocent blood, . . . —Prov 6:16-17

REFLECTION. Legalized abortion worldwide has
obliterated so many people that it is the equiva-
lent of having China as the only nation left, with
all the rest of the world's population gone.

The damage done already surpasses that of a
nuclear war.

PRAYER. *Lord, may we all share Your hatred of
evil and Your love for humanity.*

OCIAL injustices stood in tension to the high ideals the Founders articulated.

—"Living the Gospel of Life," 14

NOV. 6

REFLECTION. The founding fathers of our nation were religious men, many of whom studied in seminaries and Bible schools. They spoke openly of Jesus, even in official government meetings.

For decades now, our courts have been removing religion and morality from public life, and we see the price we have paid in tens of millions of aborted children.

PRAYER. *Bless our nation, Lord, that it may always acknowledge You publicly as the foundation of our rights and freedom.*

O posit a right to abortion, infanticide and euthanasia, and to acknowledge it by law, is to give human freedom a perverse and wicked meaning: absolute power above and against others. At that point authentic freedom dies.

—*The Gospel of Life,* 20

NOV. 7

REFLECTION. Freedom has a meaning and a consistency; it never destroys in others what it claims for itself. So much oppression masquerades as "freedom of choice."

PRAYER. *Lord, only in You and in Your Word do we discover the power of freedom.*

RELIGION that God our Father accepts as pure and undefiled is this: to come to the aid of orphans and widows in their hardships. . . . —Jas 1:27

NOV. 8

REFLECTION. When Roe v. Wade permitted abortion, it said, "The word *person* as used in the 14th Amendment does not include the unborn." It was a statement of exclusion and intolerance, of prejudice and marginalization.

We, in contrast, have our arms open wider to expand the circle of welcome into the human family. Pro-life people are the more tolerant ones.

PRAYER. *Lord, break down the walls of prejudice that would exclude anyone from our protection and love.*

HE will free them from oppression and violence, for their blood is precious in His sight. —Ps 72:14

NOV. 9

REFLECTION. This psalm foretells the Messiah and describes the effects of His coming.

The Messiah holds the blood of human lives as precious, and therefore He brings an end to oppression and violence. He is on the side of the helpless.

PRAYER. *Lord, may we praise You, the God Who sets us free from violence, and cooperate with Your grace to free the oppressed.*

N this mountain He will destroy the shroud that enfolds all peoples, the sheet that covers all nations; He will swallow up death forever. —Isa 25:7-8

NOV. 10

REFLECTION. God did not make death. He hates it, and in fact has fulfilled this ancient promise of Isaiah through the death and Resurrection of Christ by which He destroyed death and made us the People of Life.

Those who continue God's work in the world, therefore, fight against the lingering power of death's kingdom, in whatever form it takes.

PRAYER. *Lord, thank You for the hope and joy of this promise that You gave through Isaiah and fulfilled in Christ.*

 OE to those who call evil good, and good evil, who put darkness for light, and light for darkness. —Isa 5:20

NOV. 11

REFLECTION. The Holy Spirit, the Spirit of Truth, shows us the truth about our sins (Jn 16:8). In Him we come to understand the difference between good and evil. This works directly against the dynamics of the abortion movement, which identifies a moral evil as a "right."

Devotion to the Holy Spirit is a key element in a Culture of Life.

PRAYER. *Come, Holy Spirit, convert the minds and hearts of all those who defend abortion.*

THE Lord said to me: "Son of man . . . confront them with their detestable practices, for . . . blood is on their hands . . . they even sacrificed their children, whom they bore." —Ezek 23:36-37

NOV. 12

REFLECTION. The pro-life movement did not begin with Roe v. Wade. It began the first time a human being extended his hand to help another. It continued as Old Testament prophets preached against child sacrifice, and as Christians in the Roman Empire rescued abandoned infants.

It continues today and it will be victorious, just as surely as Christ is Risen!

PRAYER. *Keep us standing, Lord, in the great tradition of life!*

VOICE is heard in Ramah, mourning and great weeping, Rachel weeping for her children and refusing to be comforted, because her children are no more. —Jer 31:15

NOV. 13

REFLECTION. A woman wrote of her abortion, "I had a severe emotional collapse. I was thinking of killing myself. I cried every day for a year or more. I did not get along with anyone too well. I felt like I hated the world. I suffered nightmares. Every time the vacuum was used I thought about how my baby died."

PRAYER. *Lord, receive the tears of so many who cry for their aborted children; may we comfort and console them.*

THE ministry of the Gospel of Life…is a precious opportunity . . . for joint efforts with Christians of other denominations . . . and with those who profess other religions and all people of good will.

NOV.
14

—*The Gospel of Life,* 91

REFLECTION. If your child needed emergency medical attention, you would cooperate with the medical technicians, no matter what their religion, to save the life of your child.

Isn't it only right, then, to cooperate with people of a different religion in order to save the life of someone else's child?

PRAYER. *Lord, give us the wisdom to cooperate with everyone in the fundamental task of saving lives.*

WICKED people and imposters will grow ever worse, deceiving others and being themselves deceived.

NOV.
15

—2 Tim 3:13

REFLECTION. Euthanasia advocates try to paint Terri Schiavo's death as peaceful, gentle and dignified. They are selling death as a product, as a better alternative than a life of suffering.

But Terri, when dying, had a look of terror and sadness on her face. In no way was this death gentle, peaceful, or dignified.

PRAYER. *Forgive Your people, Lord, and free us from deception.*

IFE is always a good . . . In what way is life a good? . . . Life, which is handed on to us by God . . . stands out amidst the world as a revelation of God, a sign of His presence, a trace of His glory.

NOV.
16

—*The Gospel of Life*, 34

REFLECTION. Abortion advocates say that the embryo or fetus is "just a collection of cells." But this is no argument at all. The same can be said of you and me.

If someone does not see the dignity of the human person, their view of people is just reduced to cells.

PRAYER. *Fill us with wonder, Lord, at Your glory shining through every human life.*

 O not do anything that endangers your neighbor's life. I am the Lord.

NOV.
17

—Lev 19:16

REFLECTION. A woman who saw the photos of aborted babies on the Priests for Life website wrote to us, "I am 17 years old and I once was pro-choice, but now I am definitely pro-life because what is happening out there is nothing less than murder.

"All women should know the facts before even contemplating an abortion."

PRAYER. *Lord, so many who do violence against life do not know the facts that can save that life. Show me many more ways to share the truth effectively.*

167

Y His Incarnation the Son of God has united Himself in some fashion with every person. —*Gaudium et Spes*, 22

REFLECTION. God has joined all humanity to Himself in Christ. There is only one human nature, shared by all human beings born and unborn, healthy and sick, rich and poor, wanted and unwanted.

Every one of these human beings is joined to God through the Incarnation, which means our humanity has a sacred value even greater than it received just by being created.

PRAYER. *Thank You, Lord Jesus, for taking upon Yourself our human nature and for uniting our human family in Yourself.*

 HIS is what the Lord says: "For three sins of Ammon, even for four, I will not turn back my wrath. Because he ripped open the pregnant women of Gilead in order to extend his borders." —Am 1:13

REFLECTION. As the University of Detroit Law Review pointed out in a 1990 article, "The Supreme Court's decisions . . . allowed abortion on demand throughout the entire nine months of pregnancy."

An abortionist may kill a healthy baby of a healthy mother right up to and including her delivery date. Indeed, Roe v. Wade is extreme.

PRAYER. *Lord, bless our efforts to educate people about what "legal abortion" really means.*

FROM the beginning you have heard the message that we should love one another, unlike Cain who was from the evil one and slew his brother. —1 Jn 3:11-12

NOV.
20

REFLECTION. When an unborn child is diagnosed with a terminal illness, some feel justified in aborting the child. The excuse they use is that he or she "will die anyway." But we will *all* die anyway.

Since when does our mortality make us disposable? Since when is the inevitability of death a justification to kill?

PRAYER. *Lord, teach us that the beauty of life is not measured in days or years, but in the love we give and receive.*

WILL fear no evil, for You are at my side. —Ps 23:4

NOV.
21

REFLECTION. Some think Congress should never have intervened in the Terri Schiavo case. Either they are unaware of the details of the case, or of the purpose of government.

Terri, although brain injured, did not have any terminal illness, was not on any form of life support, and did not require any medications to stay alive. Some did not believe her life was worth living. So what is the government supposed to do when some citizens try to kill another citizen?

PRAYER. *Bless our leaders, Lord, with the courage to protect our lives.*

E will wipe every tear from their eyes, and there will no longer be death.
—Rev 21:4

NOV. 22

REFLECTION. Men continue to suffer from the abortion of their children. Many of them repent of having shed the blood of the person God entrusted to their care, love, and protection.

Others tried to protect their child, and were not allowed by the child's mother or by the law to intervene to stop the abortion. Men in these circumstances need to know that they do not weep alone and that healing is available.

PRAYER. *Redeem, O Lord, the fathers whose hearts are torn by the abortion of their children.*

 OUR hands are full of blood; wash and make yourselves clean. Take your evil deeds out of my sight! Stop doing wrong, learn to do right! —Isa 1:16

NOV. 23

REFLECTION. Some abortion advocates agree that abortion should be "reduced." The pro-life movement does reduce abortions, but also works to end it, and this is what the other side considers "divisive." They want to present themselves as favoring life, but they don't want to protect every life.

It's like saying we should reduce child abuse but that trying to prohibit it altogether is divisive.

PRAYER. *Lord, continue to divide good from evil as You work through us.*

HILE there are differences in nature and moral gravity, contraception and abortion are often linked as fruits of a single tree.

—*The Gospel of Life*, 13

REFLECTION. Contraception is more like the sister to abortion than the parent.

Pope John Paul II continues, "Such practices are rooted in a hedonistic mentality unwilling to accept responsibility in matters of sexuality, and they imply a self-centered concept of freedom, which regards procreation as an obstacle to personal fulfillment."

PRAYER. *Lord, free us from the bitter fruits of a false idea of freedom and procreation.*

 NY politics of human life must work to resist the violence of war and the scandal of capital punishment. Any politics of human dignity must seriously address issues of racism, poverty, hunger, employment, education, housing, and health care.

—"Living the Gospel of Life," 23

REFLECTION. Care for human life is multifaceted.

Although we can't do everything, we have concern for all people, and we realize that progress in any area of human dignity facilitates progress in every other area.

PRAYER. *Lord, as progress is made for human rights, may all people, born and unborn, reap the benefit.*

KINGDOM of truth and life, a kingdom of holiness and grace, a kingdom of justice, love, and peace. . . .

—Preface, Liturgy of Christ the King

REFLECTION. Jesus is Lord, not only of individuals, but of nations and the entire universe. All history finds its fulfillment in Him.

The Dominion of Christ over all creation is shown in the fact that He has conquered death. That is why His followers are pro-life. They bear witness to His Kingdom and look forward to His Second Coming.

PRAYER. *Lord Jesus, continue to extend Your victory over death through the work of Your disciples.*

HEN you spread out your hands in prayer, I will hide My eyes from you; even if you offer many prayers, I will not listen. Your hands are full of blood. —Isa 1:15

REFLECTION. Some abortion advocates call themselves "Prayerfully pro-choice." The implication is that they have consulted God about a procedure that dismembers little babies and found it to be OK. This is using faith against reason.

The God who gives us faith also gives us common sense. Nothing that truly comes from God is ever going to tolerate the killing of innocent human beings.

PRAYER. *Lord, may we never use our religion to justify sin.*

IKE a boil that can never be cured so long as it is covered up but must be opened with all its ugliness to the natural medicines of air and light, injustice must be exposed, . . . to the light of human conscience and the air of national opinion before it can be cured.

NOV.
28

—Dr. Martin Luther King, Jr.,
"Letter from Birmingham Jail," April 1963

REFLECTION. The injustice of abortion is hidden. We must expose it through pictures and descriptions of the procedure and testimonies of those wounded by it.

PRAYER. *Lord, You are the light that exposes darkness. May we expose and overcome evil.*

O anyone who is victorious, I will give the right to sit with Me on My throne.

NOV.
29

—Rev 3:21

REFLECTION. When Milwaukee police found children throwing things off a bridge one day and asked what they were throwing, they answered, "Little people." The police then saw the small containers of tiny babies that had been aborted in a nearby abortion clinic and left in the garbage bin.

The destiny of the human person is the heights of heaven. That's why we can't ignore it when people are thrown in the garbage.

PRAYER. *Lord, may Your awesome promise to humanity inspire our pro-life efforts.*

OD greatly increased the number of His people and made them too strong for their foes. —Ps 105:24

NOV. 30

REFLECTION. Dr. Joseph Chamie, Director of the Population Division at the United Nations, has said, "A growing number of countries view their low birth rates with the resulting population decline and ageing to be a serious crisis, jeopardizing the basic foundations of the nation and threatening its survival."

Keep this in mind the next time someone talks to you about over-population.

PRAYER. *Lord, continue to make Your people fruitful. Bless all nations with the gift of life and the joy of welcoming it.*

 HE program of Jesus is "a heart which sees." This heart sees where love is needed and acts accordingly. —Pope Benedict XVI, *God is Love*

DEC. 1

REFLECTION. One of the first things you can do to stop abortion is to be sure you know a phone number that people can call for alternatives to abortion and healing after abortion.

The national hotline number 1-800-395-HELP connects people to both kinds of help nearest to where they live. Promote this number in any way you can!

PRAYER. *Father, make me ready to point people to where they can find help, and courageous to speak up when they need it.*

" **R**ESTRAIN your voice from weeping and your eyes from tears" . . . declares the Lord. . . . "There is hope for your future."
—Jer 31:16-17

DEC. 2

REFLECTION. A woman writes of her abortion, "It was gruesome. I looked over and could see body parts floating in a sea of blood. I was ten weeks pregnant. The canister was right next to my head. I screamed and the nurse covered it.

"It changed my life forever. I could never look at children after that without crying."

PRAYER. *Lord, send repentance and forgiveness to all who have had abortions. Hear their cries; fill them with new hope.*

NO one can tame the tongue. . . . With it we bless the Lord and Father, and with it we curse people who are made in the likeness of God.
—Jas 3:8-9

DEC. 3

REFLECTION. In the efforts to oppress various segments of humanity, dehumanizing language is always used. The unborn have been called "parasites," "tissue," and other non-personal names.

Such language not only degrades persons but dishonors the One who made them in His image. The Culture of Life demands language that ennobles and honors.

PRAYER. *Guard our tongues, Lord God, that what we say about human lives may always honor them and You.*

175

YOU also must be prepared, because the Son of Man will come at an hour when you do not expect Him.   —Mt 24:44

DEC.
4

REFLECTION. The word "Advent" means "coming," and the season focuses on the coming of Christ at the end of time, and then on His first coming at Christmas.

The joy of Advent is joined by a strong warning that we must be prepared for His coming. Promoting justice and human rights is a key element of our preparation. A society that aborts its children is not prepared for the coming of Christ.

PRAYER. *Come, Lord Jesus. May we be prepared to welcome You by welcoming all human life.*

THE dawn from on high will break upon us to shine on those who sit in darkness and the shadow of death.   —Lk 1:78-79

DEC.
5

REFLECTION. A woman who saw the photos of aborted babies on the Priests for Life website wrote to us, "I have always thought that it should be a woman's right to do what she wanted to her body. Today I stand corrected. Thank you for showing me the truth. I will pray for success in your fight against abortion."

PRAYER. *Guide us, Lord, that we may see life as You see it and help others do the same.*

HE will come again in glory to judge the living and the dead.

—Nicene Creed

DEC. 6

REFLECTION. Advent focuses us on the Second Coming of Christ. He will return to earth, separate good from evil entirely, and publicly judge every person who ever lived. All the good we have done, especially at the price of ridicule, will be rewarded publicly.

In the light of His coming, what sacrifice is too great to make for our smallest brothers and sisters?

PRAYER. *Lord, remove my fear of ridicule for standing up for what is right. May the light of Your coming strengthen my pro-life witness.*

LET there arise to God the Creator a heartfelt and worldwide prayer on behalf of life.

—*The Gospel of Life*, 100

DEC. 7

REFLECTION. Prayer is the opposite dynamic of "pro-choice" or "choice to die," because those ideas assert the primacy of the individual, while prayer acknowledges the primacy of God.

Prayer for life, moreover, does not simply ask God to end the culture of death but commits us to be active in fighting for the vulnerable.

PRAYER. *Lord, unite Your people in praise and thanksgiving for life, in repentance for taking it, and in supplication for protecting it.*

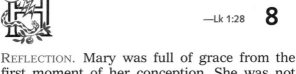

HAIL, full of grace. The Lord is with you.

—Lk 1:28

DEC.

8

REFLECTION. Mary was full of grace from the first moment of her conception. She was not exempt from the need of a Savior; He simply shared with her in a unique way the victory over sin that He offers all of us.

For those tempted to abort, there is always sufficient grace to do what is right.

PRAYER. *Mary, pray for us and for all tempted to abort, that they may say yes to life.*

MARY, brilliant dawn of the world renewed, Mother of all the living, we commend to you the entire cause of life. —*The Gospel of Life*, 105

DEC.

9

REFLECTION. When Our Lady of Guadalupe appeared to Juan Diego (whose feast is today), the Aztecs were practicing human sacrifice.

Mary's image brought the message that God was with them—so much, in fact, that He became a child, carried in Mary's womb. This gave them hope, and they stopped their human sacrifice and became Christian.

PRAYER. *Saint Juan Diego, pray for us. Our Lady of Guadalupe, pray for us.*

HE hired hand . . . sees the wolf approaching, and he leaves the sheep and runs away, while the wolf catches and scatters them. —Jn 10:12

DEC. 10

REFLECTION. The pro-life struggle is not about a mother against her baby. It is about mother and baby together against a destructive and unscrupulous abortion industry that cares for neither.

To be pro-life is to be pro-woman, and to ask, "Why can't we love them both?"

PRAYER. *Lord, make us good shepherds, like You are, that we may stand for the vulnerable and protect them.*

 OR He will save the poor who cry out and the needy who have no one to help them. —Ps 72:12

DEC. 11

REFLECTION. When God works among His people, He overcomes isolation, division, and abandonment. He is the God who gathers together, unites, and bonds.

When there are needy people around, that problem is made worse when they "have no one to help them." That's where God comes in to make the difference by inspiring people to do something.

PRAYER. *Lord, help us to come to the aid of those who have no help and whose lives are endangered.*

179

GREAT sign appeared in heaven: a woman clothed with the sun, with the moon beneath her feet, and a crown of twelve stars on her head. —Rev 12:1

DEC.
12

REFLECTION. Our Lady of Guadalupe is the patroness of the unborn. Her image shows her as pregnant, carrying God Himself. That image converted millions of Aztecs.

Today, this image is taken to abortion clinics, where human sacrifice is practiced, and turns the despair of those mothers and fathers into the hope that brings new life.

PRAYER. *Jesus, through Our Lady of Guadalupe may we spread Your hope everywhere.*

E have come to the point where even the most common, simple forms of care are being denied.
—*The Gospel of Life*, 14

DEC.
13

REFLECTION. Some do not believe that artificial means, like feeding tubes, need to be used to provide nutrition. But every meal we have is also artificially provided. Straws and cups are artificial. So are the numerous processes by which our food comes from the fields, through the food companies and supermarkets, through ovens and microwaves, and onto our tables.

Food and water are always normal, obligatory care, even when administered in artificial ways.

PRAYER. *Lord, protect all who need assistance for the most basic provisions of life.*

HEN He went down with them and came to Nazareth, and He was obedient to them. —Lk 2:51

DEC. 14

REFLECTION. Though He was conceived of a virgin, Jesus nevertheless lived as a son in a human family. The family is the sanctuary of life. The family, above all, is where life is to be welcomed, no matter how fragile or inconvenient it may be.

One of the many reasons why the Church sees abortion and euthanasia as pre-eminent issues is because these crimes are committed by one family member upon another.

PRAYER. *O Holy Family, bless our families and lead us to a Culture of Life.*

E will govern your people fairly and deal justly with your poor ones. —Ps 72:2

DEC. 15

REFLECTION. The preparation for Christ's coming is reform; the promise of His coming is reconciliation. And the two are linked.

If the Messiah comes to restore harmony between nations and people, then the people of the Messiah are to repent of whatever destroys that harmony. If the Messiah will judge the poor with justice, then the people of the Messiah are to work to eliminate injustice.

PRAYER. *Strengthen Your people, Lord, to fight the greatest injustice of our times, which is abortion.*

NEVER again will there be in it an infant who lives but a few days . . . .They will neither harm nor destroy on all My holy mountain. —Isa 65:20, 25

DEC. **16**

REFLECTION. Christ's coming heralds a new harmony in all of nature, including between mother and child.

Advent leads us to the Silent Night when the whole world finds joy in His birth, a joy no longer threatened by violence

PRAYER. *Lord, may Your birth shed protection on all about to be born, and as we work to end abortion, may we "wait in joyful hope for the coming of Our Savior, Jesus Christ."*

 AND the Word became flesh and dwelt among us. —Jn 1:14

DEC. **17**

REFLECTION. Christmas, for which we are now preparing, is not simply the feast of the birth of Christ; it is the feast of His becoming human, the reality called the Incarnation.

Jesus was an embryo, a fetus. Life in the womb, which was already sacred because it comes from God, is now made even more holy and worthy of our every sacrifice.

PRAYER. *Lord Jesus, You lived for nine months within the body of the Virgin Mary. Give success to the efforts of all who believe in Your Incarnation to protect every life in the womb.*

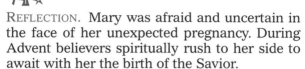

HE was greatly troubled by his words . . . **DEC.**

—Lk 1:29 **18**

REFLECTION. Mary was afraid and uncertain in the face of her unexpected pregnancy. During Advent believers spiritually rush to her side to await with her the birth of the Savior.

The best way for us to celebrate Christmas is to rush physically to the side of those in the community who, like Mary, are uncertain and afraid about their pregnancy. Let us strengthen them to choose life.

PRAYER. *Father, through the prayers of Mary, give those who are pregnant strength, and enable me to reach out to them.*

EE what love the Father has bestowed on **DEC.** us, enabling us to be called the children of God. —1 Jn 3:1 **19**

REFLECTION. St. Augustine said of Christmas, "God became man so that man might become God."

Christmas is about a wondrous exchange of natures: God shares our frail humanity, and we share His divinity.

PRAYER. *Lord, as You have given us a share in Your nature, so give us all a more profound reverence for the life of every human being!*

WHOEVER has seen Me has seen the Father.

—Jn 14:9

DEC. 20

REFLECTION. Christmas is *God in human language*. It is not simply about the birth of a child, but rather the coming of the One Who will preach the Sermon on the Mount, instruct us by parables, and establish His Church.

This is why it makes no sense to welcome the Child but reject His teachings. There can be no such thing as a "pro-choice Christian."

PRAYER. *Jesus, in welcoming You I welcome the Father and all the truth and grace He gives us through You!*

———————

I WILL come again and will take you to Myself, so that where I am, you may also be.

—Jn 14:3

DEC. 21

REFLECTION. Christmas means more than kindness, family, joy, and giving. It's about what kind of destiny awaits us beyond the grave.

Christmas is about the Gospel of Life, the hope of eternal life offered through the birth of a Child Whom we accept by faith. In the light of the manger, we see every human person as one who is called to *be where Christ is in glory!*

PRAYER. *Lord, You want every human person to be where You are. Fill me with that kind of love for every life.*

E did not spare His own Son. . . . How then can He fail also to give us everything else . . . ? —Rom 8:32

REFLECTION. The song "Grown-up Christmas List" speaks of a list for a world in need. This list includes, "no more lives torn apart, that wars may never start . . . that right would always win."

Christmas is a time for wishing boldly for good things. Let us write our Christmas list with confidence.

PRAYER. *Father, increase our longing that every life may be safe from the violence of abortion and euthanasia, and from the ravages of poverty, crime, and war.*

 HERE has been born to you a Savior, Who is Christ, the Lord. —Lk 2:11

REFLECTION. From the beginning of time, prophets announced that the Messiah of the Lord would come. "Messiah," or "Christ" means "Anointed One."

On Christmas, this prophecy was fulfilled in a surprising way, because the Angels did not simply announce that Jesus was the Messiah *of the Lord*. They said the newborn child was *Messiah AND Lord*.

PRAYER. *Fill us, Lord, with the wonder of God joining our human family and raising our dignity beyond our imagination.*

E has anointed Me . . . to let the oppressed go free. **DEC. 24**

—Lk 4:18

REFLECTION. "Truly He taught us to love one another. His law is love, and His gospel is peace. Chains shall He break, for the slave is our brother, and in His name all oppression shall cease" *(O Holy Night)*.

In the name of the newborn Christ, the oppression of our unborn children will cease.

PRAYER. *Lord, may the joy of Your birth give us the strength to be more active than ever in the pro-life cause for You are Lord forever and ever.*

EHOLD, I proclaim to you good news of great joy that will be for all the people. . . . A Savior has been born for you. **DEC. 25**

—Lk 2:10-11

REFLECTION. The good news of Christmas is for everyone, and especially for the unborn, the most helpless of all.

Christ's birth was announced first to the lowly, not to the powerful. Jesus' ministry continued to follow that pattern: He consistently sought out those who were on the outskirts of society. We are called to do the same.

PRAYER. *Lord, to welcome You means to welcome the obligations that Your mission places on us. This Christmas, I resolve to intervene for the unborn child.*

HEN they saw the Child, they recounted the message that had been told them about Him.

—Lk 2:17

REFLECTION. The Shepherds saw the newborn Christ, and the message that they had heard was that He was a Savior *for all people.*

Seeing Him, they understood this even better. After all, who is more approachable than a baby? Nobody, no matter how poor or lowly, would have reason to be afraid to approach Him.

PRAYER. *Lord, You continue to reveal Yourself in the tiny babies yet in the womb. May we see You, and love You in them.*

 HE Lord . . . has manifested His righteousness for all the nations to see.

—Ps 98:2

REFLECTION. Thanks to Christmas, all the earth has seen the saving hand of God! A new and radiant vision of His glory has shone upon us, because human life has been joined to Him.

He has raised human life to a greater dignity than it had before. Life was always sacred, because it is God's creation. But thanks to Christmas, human life is forever united to Divine Life in and through the Infant King of Bethlehem.

PRAYER. *Lord, may all Your people continue to marvel at Your love for human life and reverence this gift as You do.*

HEROD . . . issued an order to kill all the boys in Bethlehem and the surrounding area who were two years old or less. —Mt 2:16

DEC. 28

REFLECTION. This Feast of the Holy Innocents leads Christians to reflect on the tragedy of abortion.

Each day, our hearts should be broken as the bodies of these babies are broken, and the souls of those who kill them are weighed down with the burden of guilt and despair.

PRAYER. *Lord, as the People of Life, enable us to bring into this world the hope that comes from the birth of Christ and from the birth of every baby.*

HE . . . laid Him in a manger, because there was no room for them in the inn. —Lk 2:7

DEC. 29

REFLECTION. The birth of Christ was planned by God from all eternity, and the details of His birth and life were announced by the Prophets. How could there be no room for Him Who owns the world and every inch of room in the whole universe?

Obviously, God did this on purpose. He wanted to show that His Son comes as a Savior to reconcile a world that is at enmity with God.

PRAYER. *Lord, as You seek room in our own hearts today, enable us to also make room for every human life.*

OME, let us go to Bethlehem to see this thing that has taken place.

—Lk 2:15

DEC. 30

REFLECTION. On Good Friday, we sing, "Were You There When They Crucified My Lord?" What if at Christmas we sang, "Were you there when the King of Kings was born?"

There is a way to be there, and it is to open ourselves to the joy and meaning of the birth of every child—to see in each child, even the unwanted and unexpected, a reflection of the Christ Who comes even today.

PRAYER. *Lord, open my heart and open every heart to the wonder of new life. May we greet You in each new child.*

ITH the Lord . . . a thousand years are like one day.

—2 Pet 3:8

DEC. 31

REFLECTION. At year's end, we reflect upon what we have done and what we have failed to do.

What have we done this year for the defense of life? Let us resolve tonight that we will increase the amount of time and energy we devote to the number one moral issue: restoring the right to life!

PRAYER. *Father, may my future be filled with the joy of life, and of defending life, through Christ our Lord.*

HOLY WEEK

PALM SUNDAY

HE crowds . . . kept shouting, "*Hosanna* to the Son of David!"

—Mt 21:9

REFLECTION. Jesus' entry into Jerusalem is triumphant, a stark contrast to the shouts of the crowd on Good Friday saying, "Crucify Him!"

The triumph of Palm Sunday represents the fact that by coming to Jerusalem, He is bringing about the triumph of grace over sin and life over death.

PRAYER. *Jesus, grant me the palm of victory to give myself away for those who cannot defend themselves.* _____

HOLY THURSDAY

F I, your Lord and Teacher, have washed your feet, you also should wash one another's feet.

—Jn 13:14

REFLECTION. On Holy Thursday, Jesus gave us the Eucharist, the Priesthood, and the commandment of charity. All are symbolized by His washing the feet of His Disciples.

We are to wash each other's feet, to do what is unpleasant in order to serve one another.

PRAYER. *Lord, I commit myself to serve my unborn brothers and sisters, just as You have served us.*

GOOD FRIDAY

THEY took Him away . . . carrying the cross by Himself. . . .

—Jn 19:16-17

REFLECTION. Jesus was not crucified because of the power of wicked men; He was crucified because of the silence of good men.

On the first Good Friday, where was the multitude who had been fed by the five loaves and two fish? Where were those who saw Lazarus come out of the tomb? Good Friday reveals the triumph of cowardice. Nobody wanted to take a risk.

PRAYER. *Crucified Lord, many betrayed You by their silence and absence. May I always speak up for You by speaking up for the vulnerable.*

HOLY SATURDAY

IN that garden there was a new tomb in which no one had ever been buried.

—Jn 19:41

REFLECTION. On Holy Saturday, the Church sits by the tomb of Christ, meditating on His death, and keeping vigil for the Resurrection.

As we fight the culture of death, let us inject the sadness of every killing with the sure hope of resurrection.

PRAYER. *Lord Jesus, amid every sorrow fill us with hope, for You live and reign forever and ever.*

191

EASTER SUNDAY

E has abolished death and brought life and immortality to light through the Gospel.

—2 Tim 1:10

REFLECTION. Jesus Christ is Risen from the dead! Death has been conquered! Although death in its various forms continues to manifest itself in our world, it has been robbed of its power; it no longer has the final word in the human story.

The pro-life movement does not simply work *for victory;* we work *from victory.* Victory is our starting point. We joyfully proclaim to the world that Christ is Risen, and that for this reason, we must choose life.

PRAYER. *Risen Lord, fill me with joy this day. May I defend life, knowing that victory has already been placed in our hands, for You are alive forevermore. Alleluia!*

OTHER OUTSTANDING BOOKS IN THIS SERIES

WORDS OF COMFORT FOR EVERY DAY—Short meditation for every day including a Scripture text and a meditative prayer to God the Father. Printed in two colors. 192 pages.   **Ask for No. 186**

LEAD, KINDLY LIGHT—By Rev. James Sharp. Minute meditations for every day of the year taken from the writings of Cardinal Newman plus a concluding prayer for each day.   **Ask for No. 184**

EVERY DAY IS A GIFT—Introduction by Most Rev. Frederick Schroeder. Popular meditations for every day, featuring a text from Sacred Scripture, a quotation from the writings of a Saint, and a meaningful prayer.   **Ask for No. 195**

JOYFULLY LIVING THE GOSPEL DAY BY DAY—By Rev. John Catoir. A beautiful book that will enable readers to live the Gospel with joy every day of the year. Each day contains a specific Scripture quotation, reflection, and prayer to encourage joyous participation in the Christian life. Printed and illustrated in two colors.   **Ask for No. 188**

MARY DAY BY DAY—Minute meditations for every day of the year, including a Scripture passage, a quotation from the Saints, and a concluding prayer. Printed in two colors with over 300 illustrations.   **Ask for No. 180**

MINUTE MEDITATIONS FROM THE POPES—By Rev. Jude Winkler, OFM Conv. Minute meditations for every day of the year using the words of twentieth-century Popes. Printed and illustrated in two colors.   **Ask for No. 175**

AUGUSTINE DAY BY DAY—By Rev. John Rotelle, O.S.A. Minute meditations for every day of the year taken from the writings of Augustine, with a concluding prayer also from the Saints.   **Ask for No. 170**

HEALING PRAYERS FOR EVERY DAY—A daily meditation book that sets forth inspiring prayers for healing of soul and body.   **Ask for No. 192**

THE HOLY SPIRIT DAY BY DAY— By Rev. Jude Winkler, OFM Conv. Contains a Scripture reading, a reflection and a prayer for every day of the year. Fr. Winkler offers us opportunity to develop a closer relationship with the Holy Spirit and apply it to our every day lives.   **Ask for No. 198**

WHEREVER CATHOLIC BOOKS ARE SOLD

ISBN 978-0-89942-168-1

90000